The Bush Theatre presents the world premiere of

tHe
dYsFUnCKshOnalZ !

by Mike Packer

14 November – 22 December 2007

Cast

Billy Abortion	**Rupert Procter**
Marc Faeces	**Ralph Brown**
John Smith	**Pearce Quigley**
Louise Gash	**Julia Ford**
Gina	**Josephine Butler**

Writer	**Mike Packer**
Director	**Tamara Harvey**
Designer	**Lucy Osborne**
Lighting Designer	**James Farncombe**
Sound Designer	**Matt McKenzie**
Composer / Musical Director	**Mia Soteriou**
Assistant Director	**Michael Oakley**
Deputy Stage Manager	**Ella May McDermott**
Stage Management Placement	**Amaryllis Courtney**
Production Photographer	**Nobby Clark**

tHe dYsFUnCKshOnalZ! received its world premiere performance at
The Bush Theatre, London on 14 November 2007

Rupert Procter Billy Abortion

Rupert graduated from Bristol Old Vic 1995.

Theatre includes *The Messiah* (directed by Steven Berkoff), *Last Night of Antonin Artaud* (Duncan Ward), *Take* (Andrew Neil) and *Serjeant Musgrave's Dance* (Elizabeth Newberry).

Film includes *Bigga Than Ben* (directed by Suzie Halewood), *Strange Little Girls* (Savina Dellicour), *The Calcium Kid* (Alex De Rakoff), *Short* (Waris Islam), *Little Clumps of Hair* (Jim Hoskin), *One for the Road* (Chris Cook), *Pure* (Gillies Mackinnon), *Domestic* (Suzi Ewing), *Heartlands* (Damien O'Donnell), *The Lowdown* (Jamie Thraves), *Shifting Units* (Chris Cook), *Notting Hill* (Roger Michel), *Regeneration* (Gillies Mackinnon) and *The Last Enemy* (Iain McDonald)

TV includes *Strictly Confidential* (directed by Roberto Bangura & Keith Boak), *Inspector Lynley* (Jonathan Fox Bassett), *Silent Witness* (Martyn Friend), *Dalziel and Pascoe* (Gwennan Sage), *The Somme* (Car Hindmarch), *Planespotting* (Chris Menaul), *Line in the Sand* (James Hawes), *Gunpowder, Treason and Plot* (Gillies MacKinnon), *Keen Eddie* (Alan Taylor), *Lenny Blue* (Andy Wilson), *A Line in the Sand* (James Hawe), *Pure Wickedness* (Harry Hook), *Peak Practice* (Ken Grieve), *Ultraviolet* (Joe Ahearne), *City Central* (Sally Aprahamian), *The Orchard Walls* (Gwennan Sage), *Kavanagh QC* (Charles Beeson), *Staying Alive* (James Hawes), *Sharman* (Matthew Evans), *Band of Gold* (Matthew Evans), *No Bananas* (Bob Tronson) and *Cardiac Arrest* (Peter Mullin).

Ralph Brown Marc Faeces

Theatre includes *Return to the Forbidden Planet* (Tricycle), *Panic* (Royal Court), *Macbeth* (Liverpool Everyman), *Deadlines* (Joint Stock) and *West* (Donmar).

TV includes *Cape Wrath* (C4), *Life on Mars* (BBC), *Cold Blood 2*(ITV), *Nearly Famous* (E4), *Flood* (ITV), *Nighty Night* (BBC3), *Coronation Street* (ITV), *Spooks* (BBC), *Big Dippers* (ITV), Lawless (ITV), *The Agency* (CBS), *Lenny Blue* (BBC), *NCS* (BBC), *Waking the Dead* (BBC), *The Lock* (C4) *Extremely Dangerous* (ITV), *Last Train* (ITV), *Cleopatra* (TNT), *Respectable Trade* (BBC), *Ivanhoe* (BBC), *Place of the Dead* (BBC), *Karaoke* (BBC), *Dalziel and Pascoe*(BBC), *Devil's Advocate* (BBC), *Say Hello to the Real Doctor Snide* (C4), *Rules of Engagement* (ITV), *A Curious Suicide* (ITV), *The Black and Blue Lamp* (BBC), *The Bill – Series 2* (ITV) *West* (C4), *Merry Wives of Windsor* (BBC), *Coppers* (BBC), *Piggybank* (C4), *Van Der Valk* (Thames) and *Christabel* (BBC).

Film includes *Bridge of Lies*, *The Shooter*, *Straightheads*, *Stoned*, *The Puritan*, *Exorcist: Dominion*, *I'll Be There*, *Mean Machine*, *The Last Run*, *The Final Curtain*, *New Year's Day*, *Star Wars: The Phantom Menace*, *Amistad*, *Up 'un' Under*, *Wayne's*

World 2, Psychotherapy, Undercover Blues, The Crying Game, Alien III, Impromptu, Diamond Skulls, Buster, Scandal, Withnail & I.

Writing includes Sanctuary (Joint Stock Theatre) Winner Samuel Beckett Award 1997, New Year's Day (Feature Film) Winner Raindance Film Festival 2002. Ralph plays keyboards and alto sax in The Brighton Beach Boys, and piano in Butterfly McQueen. Ralph would like to thank Stephen Wrigley, Rory Cameron and Adrian Marshall for teaching him the guitar.

Pearce Quigley John Smith

Pearce's theatre credits include: *The Seagull* (Royal Court); *Paul* (National); *Journey's End* (Comedy Theatre); *My Night With Reg* and *Dealers Choice* (Birmingham Rep); *Feelgood* (Hampstead and Garrick); *Blue Heart* (Royal Court); *Shopping and F**king* (Out of Joint at Gielgud, International Tour and Queen's Theatre); *The Queen and I - The Royals Down Under* (Out of Joint Australian Tour); *Rat in the Skull* (Royal Court and Duke of York's); *The Queen and I* (Out of Joint at The Royal Court & Vaudeville Theatre); *Road* (Out of Joint at Royal Court), *Der Neue Menoza* (Gate Theatre), *Rope* (Birmingham Rep), *A Jovial Crew* (RSC); *A Winter's Tale* (RSC); *Merry Wives of Windsor* (RSC); *The Changeling* (RSC); *The Pied Piper*; *Lives of the Great Poisoners*; *Hot Fudge and Ice Cream*; *Etta Jenks*; *Abingdon Square* (Shared Experience).

His television credits include: *Lead Balloon*; *Riot at the Rite*; *Cutting It* (Series 1-4); *Big Dippers*; *15 Storeys High*; *Happiness* (Series 1 & 2); *Pay & Display*; *Queer As Folk*; *A Big Bunch of Hippies*; *That Peter Kay Thing*; *How to Love in the 21st Century*; *Two Minutes*; *Pie In the Sky*; *Prime Suspect*; *Growing Rich*; *A Perfect Hero*; *Ladder of Swords*; *Killing Dad*; *Inspector Morse*.

Recent films include: *Grow Your Own* (Warp Films); *Born Equal* (BBC Films); *Millions* (Mission Pictures); *House of Mirth* (3 Rivers for FilmFour).

Julia Ford Louise Gash

Julia has worked at The Bush twice before, in *The Chinese Wolf* and *Adrenalin Heart*.

She trained at BOVTS. Theatre credits include: *The Life of Galileo, Piano, The Crucible, School for Wives, Yerma* (National Theatre); *The Weir, Some Singing Blood* (Royal Court); *The Lodger, Now You Know* (Hampstead); *Hamlet* (Riverside Studios and Tour); *Venus and Adonis* (Almeida); *The Lodger, Two Clouds Over Eden* (Royal Exchange, Manchester); *The*

Plantagenets, Much Ado About Nothing, King John (RSC); *Two Wheel* (Tricycle); *Duchess of Malfi, Midsummer Night's Dream* (Contact Theatre Manchester); *A Doll's House, Who's Afraid of Virginia Woolf* (Wolsey Ipswich); *Touched, Accrington Pals, Railway Children* and *Clowns On A School Outing* (Oldham).

Film includes *Summer, A Room For Romeo Brass, Wondrous Oblivion*, The Cinematic Orchestra Music Promo *Breathe, Shadowman, Moth, Butterfly World, Soft Sand Blue Sea*.

TV includes *Coming Down The Mountain, The Street Series 2, Mutual Friend, The Good Samaritan, All About George, Island At War, Anchor Me, In A Land of Plenty, A Skirt Through History, Insiders, The Healer, Birthday Girl, Best Friends, The Chemistry Lesson, Eight Hours From Paris, Fergus's Wedding, A Fatal Inversion, The Ritz, Waking The Dead, Medics, Casualty, Silent Witness, The Bill, Midsomer Murders, Strike Force, Merrihill Millionaires, Bergerac, The Practice* and *Where The Heart Is*. Radio includes *Five Kinds of Silence, Five Letters home to Elizabeth, Remains of the Day*, The *Small House at Allington, Samuel Pepys, The Fancy Man*.

She has directed two short films. *The Enlightenment* (Finalist Kodak/Bafta Short Film Showcase 2006) and *A Man Sat Next To Me...* (For The Lewisham Film Initiative) and has just directed *Let Sleeping Girls Lie* at Arts Educational (The BA Final Years Acting Students).

Josephine Butler Gina

Theatre includes *Moonlight and Magnolia* (Tricycle); *Going to the Chapel* (Salisbury Playhouse); *The Drowned World* (Traverse/The Bush Theatre); *Hock and Soda Water* (Chichester); *The Blue Room, Watching the Sand from the Sea* (Derby Playhouse) and *Ghost Sonata* (Gate Theatre).

Film includes *January 2nd* (January Films); *The Lawless Heart* (MP Productions); *Shiner* (Wise Croft Films); *Out of Depth* (Steon Films); *Up Stood the Ape* (Dumdum Fiilms) and *Nuclear Train* (MP Productions).

TV includes: *Spooks* (Kudos); *Perfect Day* (Channel Five); *Sorted* (BBC); *Happy Valley* (Touchpaper TV); *The Tunnel of Love* (LWT); *Lie With Me* (Granada); *Grass* (BBC); *Fifteen Storeys High* (BBC); *Second Sight* (BBC); *Highlander: The Raven* (Gaumont TV); *Blonde Bombshell* (LWT); *Mr White Goes to Westminster* (Hat Trick); *The Vanishing Man* (ABTV); *Ruth Rendell Mysteries: Going Wrong* (Meridian); *The Grand* (Granada); *Wycliffe* (HTV); *Dalziel and Pascoe* (BBC).

Mike Packer Writer

Previously an actor. Mike worked extensively in theatre and television.

tHe dYsFUnCKshOnalZ! is Mike's third play for The Bush. His first play, *To Live Like a King* was a runner up for the Allied Domecq New Playwrights Award. His second, *Cardboys*, was staged at The Bush in 1999. *A Carpet, a Pony and a Monkey* opened at The Bush in May 2003. Mike's screenplays include *Sixteen Thousand Toots* and *Card Boys*.

Tamara Harvey Director

Most recently, Tamara has directed new plays by Mark Ravenhill and Lucy Kirkwood for the Terror Season at the Union Theatre. Further theatre credits include: *Touch Wood*, *Purvis*, *Storm in a Tea Chest* and *The Prodigal Son* (all premieres, Stephen Joseph Theatre, Scarborough); *Closer* (Theatre Royal, Northampton); *One Flew Over the Cuckoo's Nest* (co-directed with Terry Johnson; Assembly Rooms, Edinburgh, West End 2005 & 2006, UK Tour 2007); *Whipping It Up* (directed for the West End from the original Bush production directed by Terry Johnson); *Bash* (Trafalgar Studios); *An Hour and a Half Late* (UK premiere, Theatre Royal Bath & UK Tour); *The Importance of Being Earnest* (Shakespeare Theatre of New Jersey, USA); *Much Ado About Nothing* (Shakespeare's Globe); *Who's the Daddy?* (premiere, King's Head Theatre, London); *The Strangeness of Others* and *Odysseus* (RADA); *Sitting Pretty* (Watford Palace Theatre); *Romeo and Juliet* and *The Golden Ass* (University of South Florida, USA); *Markings* (premiere, Southwark Playhouse & Traverse, Edinburgh); *The Graduate* (UK Tour); *A Tempestade* (Associate Director, Teatro Sao Luiz, Portugal); *Young Emma* and *Something Cloudy, Something Clear* (UK premieres, Finborough Theatre, London); *La Traviata* (co-revival director, English Touring Opera); *Lovers* and *Fourteen Hundred Thousand* (New York Performance Alliance, USA) and *The Lion, the Witch and the Wardrobe* (Maitisong, Botswana). Tamara is a graduate of the University of Bristol and trained at the Shakespeare Theatre of New Jersey, USA.

Lucy Osborne Designer

Lucy trained at the Motley Theatre Design School and her designs include *Rope* (Watermill Theatre), *Closer* (Theatre Royal Northampton), *Touch Wood* (Stephen Joseph Theatre), *Breaker Morant* (Udderbelly, Edinburgh Festival), *Ship of Fools* (set, Theatre 503), *The Long and the Short and the Tall* (Sheffield Lyceum and Tour), *Dr Faustus* (The Place), *Richard III* (Cambridge Arts Theatre), *The Tempest* (set, Box Clever national tour), *The Prayer Room* (Edinburgh International Festival and Birmingham Rep), *Flight Without End, Othello, Lysistrata* (LAMDA), *Season of Migration to the North* (RSC New Work Festival), *Almost Blue,* the winner of the Oxford Samuel Beckett Trust Award (Riverside Studios), *The Unthinkable* (Sheffield Crucible Studio) and Generation (Gate Theatre, Notting Hill). Future projects include *Be My Baby* for the New Vic Theatre and *Some Kind of Bliss* at the Trafalgar Studios.

James Farncombe Lighting Designer

Credits include *Life After Scandal, Taking Care of Baby, Blonde Bombshells of 1943, Nathan The Wise, Osama The Hero, A Single Act* and *The Maths Tutor* (Hampstead Theatre, London); *Three Sisters* and *Forward* (Birmingham Rep); *Blest Be The Tie* and *What's In The Cat* (Royal Court, London); *Crooked* and *I Like Mine With a Kiss* (The Bush Theatre London); *Improbable Fiction, Touch Wood, Making Waves* and *Soap* (Stephen Joseph Theatre, Scarborough); *Blues For Mr. Charlie* (Tricycle and Ipswich Wolsey); *Blues in the Night, A Funny Thing Happened on the Way to the Forum* and *Vincent in Brixton* (New Wolsey, Ipswich); *I Have Been Here Before* and *Beautiful Thing* (Nottingham Playhouse); *Dead Funny* and *Abigail's Party* (York Theatre Royal); *Sing Yer Heart Out for the Lads, Lord Of The Flies, Looking for JJ, The Twits* and *Bloodtide* (Pilot Theatre Company); *Accidental Death Of An Anarchist, A View From The Bridge, What the Butler Saw, The Hypochondriac* (nominated Manchester Evening News Awards Best Design Team 2003), *Dead Funny, Popcorn* and *Improbable Fiction* (The Octagon, Bolton); *To Kill A Mockingbird, Master Harold And The Boys, West Side Story, Death Of A Salesman, Peter Pan, The Witches, Plague Of Innocence* and *Unsuitable Girls* (Leicester Haymarket Theatre); *High Heel Parrotfish, Urban Afro Saxons* and *Funny Black Women On The Edge* (Theatre Royal, Stratford East); *Called to Account* and *Playboy Of The West Indies* (Tricycle and Nottingham Playhouse); *This Lime Tree Bower* (The Belgrade Coventry); *Hysteria* (Exeter Northcott); *Amy's View* (Salisbury Playhouse and Royal Theatre, Northampton); *Krapp's Last Tape, The Kiss, A Different Way Home* (Lakeside Arts, Nottingham); *Hang Lenny Pope, Street Trilogy* and *Cloudburst* (Theatre Absolute); *The Blue Room* and *The Elephant Man* (Worcester Swan Theatre); *East Is East* and *A Women Of No Importance* (New Vic Theatre, Stoke); *Goldilocks* (Lyric Theatre, Hammersmith); *Private Fears in Public Places, Speed-the-Plow, A Day In The Death Of Joe Egg, The Price* and *Larkin With Women* (Manchester Library Theatre).

Mia Soteriou Composer / Musical Director

Mia has combined music and acting throughout her career. As composer for theatre, work includes *Brand, A Midsummer Night's Dream* (West End), *La Lupa, The Seagull, A Midsummer Night's Dream* (RSC), *Comedy of Errors* (Globe), *Rosencrantz and Guildenstern are Dead* (RNT), *Venice Preserved* (Royal Exchange), *David Copperfield, Huckleberry Finn, Northanger Abbey, East Lynne, A Tale of Two Cities, Prisoner of Zenda, Caesar and Cleopatra* (Greenwich Theatre), *The Tempest, The Pied Piper* (Chichester), *Fat Souls* (Warehouse, Croydon), *Troilus and Cressida* (National Youth Theatre), *Daisy Pulls it Off* (Leicester). Mia was also Arranger/MD of *The Glee Club* (The Bush/West End).

As composer/actor, work for theatre includes *Comic Mysteries* (Oxford Stage Company), *Celestina* (Actors Touring Company), *Cyrano de Bergerac, The Government Inspector* (Greenwich), *Don Quixote* (Warehouse Croydon), *Spring Awakening* (Sheffield Crucible), Yoko Ono in *Lennon* (Liverpool, Sheffield and West End – also Musical Director in West End), *Bed of Roses* (Bush/Royal Court/Hull Truck).

As an actor, theatre includes roleds for the Royal Court, Bush. Lyric Hammersmith, English Touring Theatre, Shared Experience, The Gate, Stratford East, RNT and many regional theatres.

Work for TV as a composer includes *Dispatches*, *The Great Egyptians*, *Happy Cow* and *Absolutely Fabulous*. As an actor, recent TV includes *Holby City*, *EastEnders*, *The Bill* and *Like Father Like Son*.

Film work as a composer includes a live piano score for Fritz Lang's silent Classic *Woman in the Moon* and silent shorts at the ICA. As an actor film work includes David Cronenberg's *Eastern Promises*, *Mamma Mia*, *Pure*, *Topsy Turvey* and *Secrets and Lies*.

Numerous scores for radio include *Little Dorrit*, *The Odyssey*, *Hiawatha*, *The Aeneid*, *Romeo and Juliet*, *As You Like It*, *Richard III*, *The Taming of The Shrew*, *Agammemnon's Children*, *Barabbas*, *Macrune's Guevara*, *Bloody Poetry*, *Yabuhara Kengyo*, *Different States* (2 sony awards) and an opera-drama *Taking Moments/ Orpheus* (Commissioned by BBC Radio 3).

In the late 70s, Mia tried to get a record deal. She was told she wrote "really good hooks, but the lyrics were too intelligent for the current market"...

The Bush Theatre

'One of the most experienced prospectors of raw talent in Europe'

The Independent

The Bush Theatre is one of the most celebrated new writing theatres in the world. We have an international reputation for discovering, nurturing and producing the best new theatre writers from the widest range of backgrounds, and for presenting their work to the highest possible standards. We look for exciting new voices that tell contemporary stories with wit, style and passion and we champion work that is both provocative and entertaining.

With around 40,000 people enjoying our productions each year, The Bush has produced hundreds of ground-breaking premieres since its inception 34 years ago. The theatre produces up to eight productions of new plays a year, many of them Bush commissions, and hosts guest productions by leading companies and artists from all over the world.

The Bush is widely acclaimed as the seedbed for the best new playwrights, many of whom have gone on to become established names in the entertainment industry, including Steve Thompson, Jack Thorne, Amelia Bullmore, Dennis Kelly, Chloë Moss, David Eldridge, Stephen Poliakoff, Snoo Wilson, Terry Johnson, Kevin Elyot, Doug Lucie, Dusty Hughes, Sharman Macdonald, Billy Roche, Catherine Johnson, Philip Ridley, Richard Cameron, Jonathan Harvey, Conor McPherson, Joe Penhall, Helen Blakeman, Mark O'Rowe and Charlotte Jones. We also champion the introduction of new talent to the industry, whilst continuing to attract major acting and directing talents, including Richard Wilson, Nadim Sawalha, Bob Hoskins, Alan Rickman, Antony Sher, Stephen Rea, Frances Barber, Lindsay Duncan, Brian Cox, Kate Beckinsale, Patricia Hodge, Simon Callow, Alison Steadman, Jim Broadbent, Tim Roth, Jane Horrocks, Mike Leigh, Mike Figgis, Mike Newell, Victoria Wood and Julie Walters.

The Bush has won over one hundred awards, and developed an enviable reputation for touring its acclaimed productions nationally and internationally. Recent tours and transfers include the West End production of *Elling* (2007), the West End transfer and national tour of *Whipping it Up*, a national tour of *Mammals* (2006), an international tour of *After The End* (2005-6), *adrenalin... heart* representing the UK in the Tokyo International Arts Festival (2004), the West End transfer (2002) and national tour of *The Glee Club* (2004), a European tour of *Stitching* (2003) and Off-Broadway transfers of *Howie the Rookie* and *Resident Alien*. Film adaptations include *Beautiful Thing* and *Disco Pigs*.

The Bush Theatre provides a free script reading service, receiving over 1500 scripts through the post every year, and reading them all. This is one small part of a comprehensive **Writers' Development Programme**, which includes workshops, one-to-one dramaturgy, rehearsed readings, research bursaries, masterclasses, residencies and commissions. We have also launched a pilot scheme for an ambitious new education, training and professional development programme, **bushfutures**, providing opportunities for different sectors of the community and professionals to access the expertise of Bush writers, directors, designers, technicians and actors, and to play an active role in influencing the future development of the theatre and its programme.

The Bush Theatre is extremely proud of its reputation for artistic excellence, its friendly atmosphere, and its undisputed role as a major force in shaping the future of British theatre.

Josie Rourke
Artistic Director

Fiona Clark
Executive Producer

At The Bush Theatre

Artistic Director	**Josie Rourke**
Executive Producer	**Fiona Clark**
General Manager	**Angela Bond**
Literary Manager	**Abigail Gonda**
Bushfutures Co-ordinator	**Anthea Williams**
Finance Manager	**Dave Smith**
Production Manager	**Robert Holmes**
Development Manager	**Sophie Hussey**
Development Officer	**Sara-Jane Westrop**
Chief Technician	**Tom White**
Resident Stage Manager	**Christabel Anderson**
Administrative Assistant	**Maxine Pemble**
Literary Assistant	**Jane Fallowfield**
Box Office Supervisor	**Ian Poole**
Box Office Assistants	**Sarah Ives, Fabiany de Castro Oliveira, Kirsty Cox**
Front of House Duty Managers	**Kellie Batchelor, Adrian Christopher, Abigail Lunb, Glenn Mortimer, Kirstin Smith, Lois Tucker, Alicia Turrell**
Duty Technicians	**Tom White, Jason Kirk, Esteban Nunez**
Associate Artists	**Tanya Burns, Es Devlin, Chloe Emmerson, Richard Jordan, Paul Miller**
Pearson Writer in Residence	**Jack Thorne**
Press Representative	**Ewan Thomson & Giles Cooper at Borkowski**
Marketing	**Ben Jefferies at Spark Arts Marketing**

The Bush Theatre
Shepherds Bush Green
London W12 8QD

Box Office: 020 7610 4224
www.bushtheatre.co.uk

The Alternative Theatre Company Ltd. (The Bush Theatre)
is a Registered Charity number: 270080
Co. registration number 1221968
VAT no. 228 3168 73

Be There At The Beginning

Our work identifying and nurturing writers is only made possible through the generous support of our Patrons and other donors. Thank you to all those who have supported us during the last year.

If you are interested in finding out how to be involved, visit the 'Support Us' section of our website, email development@bushtheatre.co.uk or call 020 7602 3703.

Lone Star

Gianni Alen-Buckley
Catherine & Pierre Lagrange
Princess of Darkness

Handful of Stars

Joe Hemani
Sarah Phelps

Glee Club

Anonymous
Bill & Judy Bollinger
Jim Broadbent
Clyde Cooper
Sophie Fauchier
Albert & Lynn Fuss
Piers & Melanie Gibson
Tanny Gordon
Adam Kenwright
Jacky Lambert
Curtis Brown Group Ltd
Richard & Elizabeth Philipps
Alan Rickman
Paul & Jill Ruddock
John & Tita Shakeshaft
June Summerill
The Peter Wolff Theatre Trust

Beautiful Thing

Anonymous
Mrs Oonagh Berry
John Bottrill
Seana Brennan
Alan Brodie
Kate Brooke
David Brooks
Clive Butler
Matthew Byam Shaw
Justin Coldwell
Jeremy Conway
Anna Donald
Alex Gammie
Vivien Goodwin
Sheila Hancock
David Hare
Lucy Heller
Francis & Mary-Lou Hussey

Bill Keeling
Jeremy & Britta Lloyd
Laurie Marsh
Ligeia Marsh
Michael McCoy
Tim McInnerny & Annie Gosney
John Michie
David & Anita Miles
Mr & Mrs Philip Mould
John & Jacqui Pearson
Mr & Mrs A Radcliffe
Wendy Rawson
John Reynolds
Caroline Robinson
David Pugh & Dafydd Rogers
Nadim Sawalha
Barry Serjent
Brian D Smith
Abigail Uden
Barrie & Roxanne Wilson

Rookies

Anonymous
Neil Adleman
Tony Allday
Ross Anderson
Pauline Asper
Mr and Mrs Badrichani
Tanya Burns & Sally Crabb
Constance Byam Shaw
Geraldine Caufield
Nigel Clark
Alan Davidson
Joy Dean
Nina Drucker
Miranda Greig
Sian Hansen
Mr G Hopkinson
Joyce Hytner, ACT IV
Robert Israel for Gordon & Co.
Peter James
Hardeep Kalsi
Casarotto Ramsay & Associates Ltd
Robin Kermode
Ray Miles
Mr & Mrs Malcolm Ogden

Julian & Amanda Platt
Radfin
Clare Rich
Mark Roberts
David Robinson
Councillor Minnie Scott Russell
Martin Shenfield
John Trotter
Loveday Waymouth
Clare Williams
Alison Winter

Platinum Corporate members

Anonymous

Silver

The Agency (London) Ltd
Peters, Fraser & Dunlop

Bronze

Act Productions Ltd
Artists Rights Group
Hat Trick Productions
Orion Management

Trust and foundation supporters

The John S Cohen Foundation
The Earls Court and Olympia Charitable Trust
The Ernest Cook Trust
Garfield Weston Foundation
The Girdlers' Company Charitable Trust
The John Thaw Foundation
The Kobler Trust
The Martin Bowley Charitable Trust
The Mercers' Company
The Royal Victoria Hall Charitable Trust
The Thistle Trust
The Vandervell Foundation
The Harold Hyam Wingate Foundation

bushfutures
building the theatre of tomorrow...

The Bush Theatre has launched an ambitious new education, training and development programme, **bushfutures**, providing opportunities for different sectors of the community and professionals to access the expertise of Bush writers, directors, designers, technicians and actors, and play an active role in influencing the future development of the theatre and its programme.

What to look out for:

Company Mentoring
Advice and support for emerging companies seeking support and expertise from The Bush

Future Playwrights
Writing courses with Bush writers and staff, culminating in scratch showcase performances

Bush Activists
A theatre group for 16+ who will study various aspects of theatre with professional practitioners

Futures Directors
Opportunities for new directors to work with professional directors and engage with The Bush

Projects in Schools
This season The Bush is working with schools in the area and giving students access to new writing, new writers and professional directors. If you are a teacher or student, please get in touch to see how we can work with your school.

If you'd like to find out more about how to get involved, please email bushfutures@bushtheatre.co.uk or call 020 7602 3703

Mike Packer

tHe
dYsFUnCKshOnalZ !

faber and faber

First published in 2007
by Faber and Faber Limited
3 Queen Square, London WC1N 3AU

Typeset by Country Setting, Kingsdown, Kent CT14 8ES
Printed in England by CPI Bookmarque, Croydon CR0 4TD

A CIP record for this book
is available from the British Library

ISBN 978-0-571-24108-8

2 4 6 8 10 9 7 5 3 1

For Julia

Characters

Billy Abortion
lead singer

Louise Gash
bass guitar

Marc Faeces
lead guitar

John Smith
drums

Gina
American, thirties

The band members can be anywhere from
forty-six to fifty-five years old

THE DYSFUNCKSHONALZ!

In memory of Rod Hall

SCENE ONE

Lights up on a store room in a supermarket. Billy, nervy, hypersensitive, wearing supermarket overalls and name tag, counts tins of baked beans in a box. Marc, gone to seed, leather jacket, guitar earrings, skull and crossbones T-shirt, pops his head in, sees Billy, and closely watches him recording the baked bean data on a clipboard.

Marc Billy?

Billy looks up from the clipboard and sees Marc. Pause.

Fuck a duck. It is you. (*Pause.*) I'm glad to see you've come up in the world. I knew you'd fulfil your destiny one day. (*Laughs.*) We can't let the press get hold of this, credibility loss ain't the word.

Billy What d'you want?

Marc A tin of baked beans, please.

Billy What d'you want? (*Goes back to recording the baked bean data.*)

Marc You. You're a fuckin' difficult man to find.

Billy Not difficult enough.

Marc I've scoured London looking for you. I've phoned fifty-four William Blakeneys.

Billy I'm not on the phone.

Marc You're not on any electoral roll either.

Billy Who's there to vote for?

Marc I even hired a private detective for three hundred squid a week. He ended up going through the death register.

Billy I bet that was a disappointment for you.

Marc You on the run?

Billy Only from my past.

Marc D'you know how I finally tracked you down?

Billy Sniffer dogs?

Marc Our website.

Billy Webshite. Talk about rewritin' history.

Marc You're welcome to put your side of things. There's an open forum.

Billy I bet that gets a lot of hits.

Marc You'd be surprised. We've still got fans in northern Europe. And there's obviously one or two in south London as well, thank God. I put out an SOS. 'Does anyone know the whereabouts of Billy Abortion?' I'd nearly given up hope when I got an email through this morning. Jumped straight in the car and here I am, the wrong side of the river. I've got a nose bleed.

Billy What d'you want?

Marc I've got great news.

Billy You got cancer?

Marc No, slightly better than that.

Billy Aids?

Marc How does a hundred grand in your pocket sound?

Billy looks up from his clipboard

Billy What?

Marc One hundred thousand pounds.

Billy What you talkin' about?

Marc 'Plastic People'.

Billy 'Plastic People'?

Marc 'Plastic fuckin' People'.

Billy What about 'Plastic fuckin' People'?

Marc We've been offered two hundred grand for it.

Billy Fuck off.

Marc It's true.

Billy Fuck off, you cunt.

Marc Two hundred big ones.

Billy Two hundred big ones for 'Plastic fuckin' People'.

Marc Fifty-one per cent to the creative tosspot that was you. And forty-nine per cent split three ways between us lesser mortals.

Billy Bollocks.

Marc Would I raise an eyelid?

Billy We never made tuppence from it when it was in the charts. Two hundred grand?

Marc They want it for an advert.

Billy An advert?

Marc A mega-American fuckin' advert. 'Plastic People's gonna be hummed from the East Coast to the fuckin' West. It's goodbye baked beans, hello champagne.

He hands Billy a solicitor's envelope.

Give me your autograph on that and one hundred big one's'll be winging their way into what I can only imagine is your very sad bank account.

Billy Advertising what?

Marc Freedom Cards.

Billy Freedom Cards? What the fuck's that?

Marc A new credit card.

Billy A credit card?

Marc Not just any credit card. This card's the biz. It's at the cuttin' edge of new technology. In a few years' time you won't be able to move without this card. It'll be used for everything. It's gonna be a credit card, debit card, travel card, ID card, reward card, loyalty card, organ fuckin' donor card. You name it, it's gonna be used for it. And what's more, it's environmentally friendly. One per cent of all profits are goin' towards savin' the planet. Plantin' trees, stuff like that. Oh, and forget chip and pin, chip and pin's gonna be fuckin' passé. Freedom Cards are gonna work with your fingerprint. All you'll have to do is put your finger on a scanner.

Billy And Big Brother comes knockin'.

Marc What?

Billy Are they thick? How can those words be used for sellin' credit cards?

Marc That's what's brilliant about it. They're only using the chorus. And if you take the chorus on its own, it could easily be a song about the joys of shopping. (*Laughs.*)

Billy How fuckin' ironic.

Marc Well, they are Yanks. (*Laughs.*) And add this to the equation. There's talk of re-releasing the single to go with

the campaign. This could be like Levi's and The Clash.
They went mega on the back of that ad. Those cunts had
a second comin'.

Billy You have to have a first comin' in order to have a
second comin'.

Marc I'm tellin' you, we're talkin' serious marketin' here.
I've been speakin' to record companies. Gettin' a buzz
goin', there's interest. And if the single did take off, we've
gotta be ready to take advantage, follow it with The
Album.

Billy We never finished The Album. Remember?

Marc I know. But I've still got the master of every session
we ever did. There's some great stuff. We all went misty-
eyed listenin' to it last week.

Billy All? Who's all?

Marc Me, Smithy and Lou. Well, we couldn't find you,
could we? Otherwise you'd've been there. We had to
meet about rehearsin'. There's a gig.

Billy A gig?

Marc They want us to sing at the campaign launch.
Twenty grand extra. First-class air fares, five-star hotel,
six months' wages for ten minutes' work. Can't be bad.
But that's optional. If you don't want to do that, I'm
happy to take the vocals.

Billy *Never Mind the Buzzcocks.* (*Laughs.*)

Marc You saw that, did you?

Billy 'Which one used to be lead guitarist with the
Anarcho Punk Band The Dysfunckshonalz? The bald
coot? The old codger? Or the gorilla?' (*Laughs.*)

Marc Didn't bother me. I got a grand for that.

Billy Humiliation comes fuckin' cheap for some.

Marc I've got a sense of humour about myself.

Billy When did you acquire that?

Marc A month ago. When I got the call from New York.

Billy The gorilla. (*Laughs.*)

Marc Well, at least I gave you some pleasure.

Billy And you can give me some more by sticking this up your arse.

He throws the contract at Marc's feet.

Those words are mine. I wrote them in one sitting. They flowed out of me in five minutes flat, over a bowl of sulfate and a line of fuckin' cornflakes. I meant every syllable. I don't want them twisted to sell credit cards. Lovely to see you. Have a nice life. Goodbye.

Pause. Marc picks up the contract.

Marc Are you windin' me up?

Billy I hope so.

Marc I was half expectin' this. I knew you wouldn't have changed. You still have to go through the power trip motions. But we ain't got time. The ad's already made. The launch is in two weeks. That's why I've been going demented trying to find you. They've got a second-choice song lined up. If I don't deliver your signature to their hands by Monday morning, we're dumped. So stop your charade. Forget the ego games and sign the thing.

Billy For fuck sake, Marc! 'Plastic People' is about being consumed by consumerism!

Marc I know. And we all have been. You could say your words have been proved to be prophetic. Congratulations, Nostradamus.

Billy I'd rather die in the gutter.

Marc That can be arranged.

Billy I will never fuckin' sell out.

Marc 'Sell out'? Fuckin' 'sell out'? You're livin' in a fuckin' time warp. The world's moved on. The game's up. We lost. 'Selling out' ain't in the dictionary no more.

Billy It never was in yours.

Marc Everyone's at it. Even the fuckin' Pistols. They've just sold their arses. Bob Dylan and Joni Mitchell are working for fuckin' Starbucks. Who d'you think you are? King fuckin' Canute?

Billy You're trespassing.

Marc I'll trespass on your head in a minute.

Billy I'm asking you to leave.

Marc Not until you sign.

Billy Security!

Marc grabs Billy.

Marc Don't push me.

Billy Security!

Marc pushes Billy against a wall.

Marc You fuck this up and you're dead!

Billy Rape! Rape!

Marc throws Billy onto the floor.

Marc You twisted shit. I'll be back. Just pull yourself together. I'll be back.

Marc exits. Blackout.

The back entrance of the supermarket. Billy comes out and heads off.

John (*off*) Billy! Billy!

Billy turns. John – roll-up, can of Stella, charity-shop suit – enters laughing.

Billy. Billy. Eh, Billy. Look at the state, state of you. What a, what a fuckin' state.

Billy Where's your other half?

John Don't. He's out the fuckin' front.

Billy Well, tell her I've gone for a seventies perm. (*Turns to leave.*)

John Eh, wait. Wait. It's me. It's me. Don't fuckin' run from me. Fuck her, I won't, I won't fuckin' tell her. Let's sneak off for a cheeky, a cheeky fuckin' shufti.

Billy Sorry, I can't. (*Heads off.*)

John What the fuck's your fuckin' problem?

Billy turns again.

Billy Problem? I'll tell you the problem. I've got a vinyl scratch, yeah. I can't get past it. I'm stuck in a thirty-year old fuckin' groove. I keep thinkin' that what was true then must be fuckin' true now.

John What?

Billy But it ain't, is it? Apparently the world's changed, so the fuckin' truth has changed.

John The truth?

Billy I've been in a coma, ain't I?

John Coma?

Billy I've just woken up and everyone's livin' in digital supermarket heaven. And me, I'm fuckin' stuck in an analogue corner shop. I'm still thinking people have got fuckin' principles!

John Principles? Don't. Fuck. I totally fuckin' agree. I do. I fuckin' . . . I agree. In principle. Like, yeah, you know, in principle. But, you know, it's the, it's the fuckin' money, innit? I mean, you can't eat fuckin' principles, can you?

Billy You starvin'? You livin' in Africa? You got malnutrition?

John Well, no, but . . .

Billy Well, you don't have to eat your fuckin' principles then, do you?

John You're right. You're fuckin' . . . I dunno what's goin' on with the world. What's, what's goin' on with it? It's gone wrong, innit? It's all gone wrong. Let's have a drink. Come on, let's put the world to rights. Nice pub around the corner. The Ship. Nice.

Billy I'm off the booze.

John No? Really? You're jokin'?

Billy But I'm thinking' of goin' back on it.

John That's, that's the fuckin' boy. I'm the Devil, I'm the fuckin' Devil. Come on.

Billy Sorry. (*Goes to leave.*)

John Wait. Wait. Just fuckin' . . . look, look. We were just talkin' about it, yeah, just, just thinkin', it's never, never been fuckin' resolved, has it, us, us leavin' you bleedin' to death in Norway.

Billy Denmark.

17

John Denmark?

Billy Copenhagen.

John Yeah, yeah, Copenhagen. Is that, is that not in Norway?

Billy No, that's Oslo.

John Oslo? I thought that was Sweden?

Billy Norway.

John What's, what's fuckin' Sweden then?

Billy Stockholm.

John Stockholm? Did we play Stockholm?

Billy No, Gothenburg.

John Gothen . . . Gothenburg? Where's that?

Billy Sweden.

John Oh, right. And we, we played there, did we?

Billy Correct.

John Not Stockholm?

Billy No.

John Fuck. My fuckin' memory. Copenhagen, see, Copenhagen. I've got no memory of that night in Copen, Copen-fuckin'-hagen, at all.

Billy That's because you weren't there.

John No, no, I fuckin' know. But . . . where was I?

Billy I don't know.

John No. I know. Neither do I. But you know that was Lou. Lou told Marc you were dead. She, she thought she'd be up on a fuckin' murder charge. They panicked.

Billy I know the story.

John Is it that? Are you still, still fuckin' pissed off about that?

Billy Oh yeah, that's it. Well, I told you, I've been in a fuckin' coma, ain't I? I've just woken up in that hotel room with four pints of blood on the sheets. I never went through the eighties and nineties. I missed out on a wedge haircut, and girl fuckin' power. I never got to wear shoulderpads or dance around my handbag to Duran Duran. In my head Michael Jackson's still fuckin' black, Madonna's a fuckin' virgin, and Princess Di's a Welsh fuckin' drag queen!

John Alright, calm, calm fuckin' . . .

Billy For fuck sake! The idea of 'Plastic People' bein' used to sell credit cards offends my fuckin' soul! If I take the money it's like sayin' everythin' I've ever stood for is bullshit. Every word I've uttered rendered meaningless. My entire life might as well be wiped out. I won't exist. Nothin' will mean anythin'. Everythin' is worth nothin'! I am still alive! I am still here! I still stand for somethin'! I am a person, not a fuckin' commodity! There's still somethin' left in this world that does not have a price on its head! Me!

John You ain't gonna change your mind, are you?

Billy I couldn't live with myself.

John No, yeah, I know. I can't, I can't live with my fuckin' self. Not on the fuckin' social, anyway. It's, it's the fuckin' yacht, the yacht in the South of France. It's a fuckin' black, black fuckin' hole.

Billy Yeah, I've got the same problem with my Lamborghini.

John Don't. Don't fuckin' talk to me about Lamborghinis. That's, that's why I've had to move back in with my fuckin' mum.

Billy Edith's still goin', is she?

John Yeah, yeah – well, not for long. I fuckin' hope not, anyway. Cancer, riddled with it.

Billy I'm sorry.

John I moved back in to look after her, see her through the pearly gates. Thought she'd be dead in a couple of weeks – that was nine, nine fuckin' months ago. The silly fuckin' cow won't let go. I have to wipe her arse, bath her, comb, comb her fuckin' wig, put her teeth in. She should be in a hospice havin' fuckin' reflexology, aroma, aromafuckin' therapy, morphine. If I had the money, the money, the fuckin' money, I'd put her in the nobbiest hospice in . . .

Billy Yeah, well, I'm genuinely sorry. I always liked your mum.

John She really liked you.

Billy I know.

John Well, she put you up for six months, didn't she? When your dad threw you out. She put you up, fed you, shagged, shagged, fuckin' shagged you, didn't she? Didn't she, didn't she fuckin' shag you? (*Laughs.*) She sends loads, loads of fuckin' love, by the way. I told her you'd been found. She's ordered a crate, a crate of fuckin' champagne. I'd better ring her, tell her, tell her to fuckin' cancel it.

Billy I've gotta go.

John Come on, I'm the fuckin' Devil, the Devil – a cheeky half, you know you fuckin' want it.

Billy Bye, John. (*Heads off.*)

John Come here.

Billy exits. John calls after him.

I'll let you know when the funeral, the fuckin' funeral is. (*Takes out his mobile.*) Cunt. (*Makes a call.*) He's whizzed off through the car park. I couldn't stop him . . . Alright, yeah. I'm after him now. I've got him in my fuckin' sights. (*Exits.*)

SCENE THREE

Evening. A bedsit in sheltered accommodation. Billy, very drunk, bottle of JD in hand, leans against a wall to support himself. Louise, prim and proper in M&S clothing, standing by the door.

Lou Nice décor.

Billy Jasper Conran.

Lou Who Feng Shui'd it? Chairman Mao?

Billy Pol Pot.

Lou What is this place? Some sort of halfway house?

Billy Halfway to paradise. So near, yet so fuckin' far away.

Lou How come you've ended up in a place like this?

Billy Don't knock it. It's government-funded. 'Don't Care in the Community.'

Lou How've you qualified for that?

Billy 'Cos no one gives a shit about me.

Lou Why's that?

Billy Because I'm a cunt.

Lou You've always been that.

Billy I know. Ain't changed. Have you?

Lou I've just had cancer, actually. So that's had quite an effect.

Pause.

Billy Typical of you, that is. Fuckin' fashion victim. And it's so *in vogue* at the moment.

Lou Oh yeah, I'll still go to any extreme to be in with the in-crowd. I had my left tit cut off this time.

Pause.

Billy But, er . . . you're, er . . . in the clear now, are you?

Lou Yeah.

Billy Good. Great. Well . . . What's next on the list? You gonna adopt an African baby? Teach it to do fuckin' *pilates*?

Lou I wouldn't mind a drink.

Pause. Billy offers her the bottle of JD.

Have you got a glass?

Billy points to the kitchen cupboards. Lou goes over to them.

The traffic, three hours from Worthing.

Billy Ooh. Worthing. The land of the dead. D'you want a cucumber fuckin' sandwich?

Lou (*looks in a cupboard*) Love one. I'm starving.

Billy There's a three-week old lump of cheese in the fridge, and I've got twenty cans of baked beans. *Mi casa su* fuckin' *casa.*

Lou I'm on a diet, anyway.

Billy Who ain't? I'm on the Carol Vorderman detox, me.

Lou looks in another cupboard.

Is one fuckin' married?

Lou Yes.

Billy What is he? An undertaker?

Lou Financial adviser.

Billy Same thing.

Lou looks in another cupboard.

Two point two children?

Lou Nought point nought.

Billy Have you got a dog instead?

Lou How many antidepressants are you on?

Billy Right, that's enough, you can fuck off now. Go on. Shouldn't have let you in. Wasted journey. I ain't signin'. Don't waste your fuckin' breath. I ain't for sale. Especially, especially not to the fuckin' Yanks. Cunts. They think, they think they own the fuckin' world. They think they can buy anythin'. Well, not me. They can't buy me!

Lou Is that shirt Levi's?

Billy looks at his shirt.

I might agree with your sentiments, babe. But you're feedin' the enemy by wearin' their clothes. It's the world we live in. You can't have it all ways.

Billy Oxfam. I got this from Oxfam.

Lou But it's still an advert for 'em, ain't it? You've got the Levi tag. You're projectin' the image. You always used to say, if you're makin' a statement, no compromise. You've gotta go all the way.

Billy Alright. Yeah, fuck. (*Takes off his shirt.*) You're right. Boycott the cunts. I'll join the fuckin' boycott. (*Throws it on the floor.*)

Lou Your jeans, Wranglers.

Beat. Billy takes off his jeans.

Billy Yeah, alright. *No pasaràn. No* fuckin' *pasaràn.* I am the line, the line in the sand. 'Plastic People', 'Plastic People' is fuckin' . . . my fuckin' Dunkirk. (*Kicks the jeans away.*)

Lou (*of his underpants*) I hope they're Calvin Klein.

Billy checks the label.

Billy Primark.

Lou Pity.

Billy How's that? I am a Yank-free zone.

Lou Congratulations.

Billy They think everything's got a price? Not me. Those cunts reckon the market is God, don't they? It's fuckin' religious, innit? They think they're spreadin' the fuckin' Gospel. And on the eighth day God said, 'Buy, buy, buy. Sell, sell, sell.' They're fuckin' messianic about it. They don't think Jesus walks on water, they think he walks up and down fuckin' Wall Street. They think they live in the promised land, they're the fuckin' chosen people. And they've gotta spread the American fuckin' Way. Which is like, 'Have a nice day.' Have a nice day? Cunts. 'Have a nice day.' What the fuck is that about? 'Have a nice day,' says some teenage Asian on twenty pence an hour. 'Have a nice day.' Fuck off, you little cunt. I don't want a fuckin' 'Happy Meal'! Happy? Fuckin' happy? Have you ever seen anyone happy eatin' that fuckin' shit? 'Happy Meals' sponsored by Walt fuckin' Disney! Free Mickey Mouse, free Donald Duck, free Chicken Little. Free piece of shit to make your kids eat fuckin' shit! Advertisin', that's advertisin' for you, that's what adverts are for, to make people buy shit they don't fuckin' need or want. 'Happy Meals'? Fuckin' miserable meals more like. 'Dad, Dad, Dad, Dad, Dad, Dad, Dad, can I have a Happy Meal, Dad? A Happy Meal, Dad? Happy Meal, Dad. Can I have a fuckin' Happy Meal? There's a Sonic toy, there's a Pokemon toy, there's *Barney the fuckin' cuntin' Dinosaur* toy! Can I have a fuckin' Happy Meal, Dad?' Have a nice day? I'll tell you a fuckin' nice day. I'll tell you when I had a very nice day. September the eleventh. What a lovely fuckin' day that was. 11/9, not 9/11, 11/9. Did you have a nice day? I fuckin' did. Have a nice day, bosh, one-nil. Have a nice day, bosh, two-nil. How many dead? Three thousand. Is that all? Three fuckin' thousand. Bleat, bleat. What about Hiroshima? What about Vietnam? What about Iraq? What about every fuckin' single day in Africa? What about the poor who starve because of free-trade zones, and the World Bank, and globalised corporate American banditry. Oh my God, the world's changed, nothin'll ever be the same again because three thousand fat cunts are dead! Ha ha ha. Hip hip hooray. Three thousand fat cunts. Have a nice day! Go on. Go. Piss off. Leave me alone. It's 'no'. I ain't signin'. I don't want to know. So fuck off!

Pause.

Lou You've got no idea how great it is to hear you rant again. That was brilliant. You've still got it. Even if you are a burnt-out old shell livin' in a shit hole. At least you've still got the fire. And more power to you, Billy. (*Takes two glasses from the cupboard.*) Marc thinks I'm here persuadin' you. But I said to him, I said no one's ever persuaded you to do anythin'.

Billy What you here for then?

She pours two JDs.

Lou Curiosity. Were you fat? Were you bald? Were you still a nutter? Why's one of the brightest men I've ever met stackin' shelves in a supermarket?

Gives Billy a glass and toasts.

The keeper of the flame.

She downs it in one. A challenge. And pours another. Billy downs his.

Billy Keeper of the flame? Oh yeah, the keeper of the flame, that's me. I've got the torch, everyone else has got fuckin' electricity. I'm in the Dark Ages with my beacon, they're all plugged into the National fuckin' Grid. I'm here shoutin' at four walls with not a pot to piss in. What's the point of that? I'm a voice in the fuckin' wilderness. (*Drinks.*)

Lou At least you're still in contact with your soul.

Billy Soul? What's that? Fuckin' soul? I ain't got a fuckin' soul. If I have, you know what it wants? It wants what everyone else fuckin' wants. It wants a holiday in the sun, it wants to lie on a Caribbean beach drinkin' rum punch. It wants a rest from fuckin' torture. It wants enough money never to worry about it ever again. It wants a massage, a plasma TV, and a fuckin' blow job. That's what my fuckin' soul wants. My fuckin' soul wants to live a soulless fuckin' existence. And you know what else my soul wants? You know what else it wants?

Lou A Hoover?

Billy My fuckin' soul wants to be Billy Abortion again.

There, I've fuckin' said it. And it's true. My soul, more than anythin' in the world, would love, would just love to get out there and be that little cunt in the spotlight one more time. That's what my fuckin' soul is really cryin' out for.

Lou I'd love to see that myself. I always tell people you were better than Lydon.

Billy Lydon? *I'm a Celebrity*? How's he got the front? He swans around now, in LA. Pops back now and again to do a few personal appearances. He's got Jonathan Ross's nose up his fuckin' arse. Next thing he'll be sittin' on Richard and Judy's fuckin' sofa, chinwaggin' with Parky, slappin' backs with Elton. You mark my words, before the decade's out, he'll be on his knees in front of the Queen, lickin' her cunt. Arise, Sir John of fuckin' Rotten! (*Drinks.*)

Lou That'd be an investiture worth seeing.

Billy Why can he do that and I can't? I still think I'm a fuckin' terrorist, that's my problem. The only thing I've ever successfully sabotaged is myself.

Lou I'd love to be on stage with you again.

Billy Johnny Cash, Johnny fuckin' Cash, yeah.

Lou Johnny Cash?

Billy Good ole country boy. And he sung from the heart. He meant it.

Lou Where's this comin' from?

Billy His daughter. His fuckin' daughter, yeah.

Lou Where's this goin'?

Billy She's got the nod on his estate, right? She gets a call, they wanna use 'Ring of Fire' for an advert. Guess what the product is, yeah? 'Ring of Fire'. Guess what the product is?

Lou The circus?

Billy Haemorrhoid cream! Fuckin' haemorrhoid cream! How dare they! How fuckin' dare they! God bless her. God bless little Miss Cash. She said 'no'. It's a fuckin' love song. And it's a great love song. It's right up there.

Pause.

Lou Can I suck your dick?

Blackout.

SCENE FOUR

A rehearsal room. The band are in position.

Marc One, two, three, four –

They play the intro. Billy pogos like a lunatic, arrives at the microphone ready to sing and collapses out of breath onto the floor. The band stop playing. Billy gasps for air.

Lou You alright, darlin'?

The band gather around.

Marc Are you sure you're up to this?

John I thought I was unfit.

Lou Is it your asthma?

Billy No.

Lou You havin' another panic attack?

Billy No.

Lou The claustrophobia?

Billy It's my lung.

Marc Your lung?

Billy I'll be alright in a sec.

Lou What d'you mean, your lung?

Billy One of 'em's had it.

Marc You what?

Billy The other's fine.

Marc You've only got one functioning lung?

Lou What's the problem with it?

Billy Copenhagen. It's been fucked since Copenhagen. You punctured it when you stabbed me. It's not been right since. Forget it. I'm alright. I'll be fine, I just got a bit carried away, I'll cut the pogo. I'll just stand still and sing. (*Gets to his feet.*)

Marc A lead singer with one lung. I can't wait to hear this.

John I'll tell you what, though. That was alright, weren't it? The intro, for a first, first go, that was alright.

Marc It was dire. Lou, you were way too fast, and you – (*John*) you were even fuckin' faster. Has anyone got any Mogadon?

John I've not played for ten years.

Lou I've not played for twenty.

Billy I've not sung for thirty.

Marc Think of the money, Marc. Just think of the money.

John You know what we need? We need, we need a drink. Oil, oil the creative cobwebs.

He picks up a bottle of vodka from beside the drum kit.

Marc Put that down. It's ten past ten in the mornin'.

Billy That's exactly what we need, creative fuel.

Marc Oh, right. Here we go. Fuckin' Pissheads Reunited.

John I, I fuckin', I need it for the, for the fuckin' rhythm.

He swigs from the bottle.

Marc You'd have to drink the Atlantic to find the fuckin' rhythm, you would.

Billy swigs from the bottle.

Lou Me next.

Marc Oh, right. Okay. Fine. I see. I see. I fuckin' see. Cheers, Lou. If you have one I've gotta have one. Otherwise I'm the straight man again. The sensible one.

Lou takes a swig.

I refuse to play the role of the parent, thirty years on. I will not play the part of the dad. I am not the fuckin' daddy. Alright?

He takes the bottle from Lou.

I'm still a nutter too. I am still a fuckin' nutter. (*Takes a large swig.*) Are we ready now?

Hands the bottle back to John.

John The chemistry, I can feel it, the old chemistry's here. Sorry, sorry, Marc, but I've gotta do this. I went searchin' for it 'cos, well, you know, old, old times' sake. (*Takes a wrap from his pocket.*) How about a bit of the orig, original rocket fuel?

Marc Don't tell me sulfate?

John Sorry, Marc.

Marc No. Absolutely one-hundred-per-cent fuckin' no.

Billy I'll have a line.

Marc This is fuckin' insane.

Billy This is great.

Marc You've got the body of an old man, d'you want a heart attack?

Billy Make it a large one.

Lou I'm lovin' this.

Marc Fuck this. Fuck the lot of you. Drop dead. Drop fuckin' dead. I couldn't give a shit.

He exits. The others laugh like naughty kids as John chops lines of sulfate on the drum kit.

Billy Wanker.

John Oh yeah, he's still a wanker.

Lou You don't think he's really gone, do you?

Billy Him? He's sweatin' desperation. This is his last chance.

John We couldn't do it without him, though. Top, top fuckin' muso.

Billy Oh yeah, he knows how to structure noise.

Lou You always need someone like that in a band.

They all laugh.

Billy The Gorilla. (*Laughs.*)

John Yeah, the Gorilla. Fuck, the Gorilla.

They crack up.

That's, that's nearly as good as the award he got from the *Melody Maker*.

Billy He got an award?

John Classic, fuckin' classic. After, after Copenhagen, yeah. He got another band together.

Billy Marc Faeces and the Turds.

John That's right. Fuckin', fuckin' shit we were. Toured everywhere. Scuz, scuz tours. '81. (*Snorts line.*) '81, yeah. The *Melody Maker* gave him the 'Dead but Won't Lie Down' award.

> *They all crack up laughing again. Marc enters.*

Marc Alright, I'll have a large one too. I'll have a very large one. We'll see who's the fuckin' old man around here. Not me. Not fuckin' me. And hurry up. We've gotta rehearse 'Tower Block Love' after this.

Billy Why we rehearsin' that crap?

Marc In case we get an encore.

Billy Are you tryin' to embarrass us? (*Sings.*)

> Lookin' out the window
> Twenty two floors up
> I see her in a dog collar
> I'd love to knock her up.

Marc Some people think that's the best song we ever did.

Billy Who? Your mum and dad? (*Snorts line.*)

Marc What else would you suggest? 'Headin' for Oblivion'?

John Oh yes. Classic, classic.

Billy (*sings*)
> Life's shit
> I've had enough

Billy, John *and* **Lou**
    Can't love
    Don't give a fuck
    Pissed off
    Have a ruck
    Sign on
    Sniff some glue
    Headin' for oblivion to give me something to do
    Headin' for oblivion
    D'you wanna come too?
    D'you wanna come too?
    D'you wanna come too?

Marc We'd've just seen an advert full of happy shoppers. I really don't think that would be the uplifting end to the evening they're looking for.

Lou What about 'Open Wound'? (*Snorts line.*)

Marc 'Open Wound'? It should've been called 'Festerin' Sore'. It's about you two. I really don't think we should go down that particular hell hole.

Billy I vote 'Open Wound'.

Lou Me too.

John Oh God. No, no, I'm not back here, am I? I dunno. Both, both classics. I can't, too close, a hair's breadth, I fuckin' abstain.

Billy 'Open Wound' it is.

Marc Fine. Whatever. As if we're gonna get an encore with you cripples, anyway.

    Marc snorts a line.

Lou What are we wearing? We can't dress like we used to.

John I've still got my Cambridge Rapist mask.

Marc I think we can forget our old image, it's not exactly appropriate.

Billy I think it's entirely appropriate. I intend to wear my straitjacket.

Marc That's hardly surprisin'. I bet you've hardly been out of it. We're wearin' T-shirts. They're bein' supplied. Everyone on the campaign's wearing 'em.

Billy T-shirts? Hold on. What's this? They're givin' us T-shirts to wear? Don't tell me they've got corporate logos on 'em?

Marc So what if they have? It's an advert launch.

Billy I ain't wearin' no advert.

Marc You're in. You've sold out. Accept it.

Billy They bought the song. Not me.

Marc If you don't want to play the game, don't come, forget the gig. I'll take the vocals. God knows what sort of sound you'll make on one lung, anyway.

Billy Whatever sound I make it'll be better than your sub-Paul McCartney karaoke fuckin' warble.

Marc It's called singing in tune. Something you never understood.

Billy Singing in tune is for Westlife. My job is to deliver the message with meaning.

Marc The message is 'Be happy and spend money you ain't got'. If you want to deliver that with meaning, fine. If not, fuck off back to your halfway house. Now are you in or out?

Pause.

Billy Let's just do this like we used to. If you miss a few notes, so what? If you forget where you are, who gives a fuck? Just bang away, make it up, front it out to the end.

John Goose bumps. I'm gettin' fuckin' goose bumps.

Marc One, two, three, four –

Billy
Wanna buy a house and a new TV
Sit and watch people I wanna be
I wanna buy a nice new car
Get behind the wheel and feel like a star
I wanna buy a washing machine
To keep my image clean
I wanna buy a brand new me
From a corporate company
Then I'll know how to be
A pristine plastic me.

I wanna buy a personality
To present the plastic me
I wanna buy a plastic wife
Cut out the trouble and strife . . .

Billy forgets the words. He makes the odd scream to cover. One by one the band stop. Pause.

John Well if that, that weren't proof that time, time don't fuckin' exist, I don't know what is.

Blackout.

35

SCENE FIVE

New York. A hotel bar. Billy and Lou, newly kitted out in designer wear, surrounded by shopping bags, champagne in an ice bucket on their table. Billy admires himself in a mirror.

Lou You look a million dollars.

Billy The cut, that is. Quality clothing. Isn't it great? Don't it make you feel good.

Lou I've booked a massage later. You should have one.

Billy A massage? Me?

Lou Let me book you one. My treat.

Billy Fuck it. Yeah, fuck it, go on, I'll have one. Book one that'll open my fuckin' chakras, yeah. Tell 'em they've been padlocked.

Lou I'll book one with a crowbar.

Billy Yeah, and a mallet. I'll have a shiatsu with a crowbar and a fuckin' mallet, please.

Lou (*toasts*) Freedom Cards.

Billy (*toasts*) Freedom Cards.

They drink.

I'm well into mine.

Lou Don't.

Billy Five and half grand.

Lou You're a nutter.

Billy They ain't getting' it back either. They can whistle for it. What are they gonna do? Sue the iconic image at the forefront of their campaign?

Lou That restaurant was lovely.

Billy That rocket salad. Rocket? Me? Fuckin' 'ell.

Lou And I'd happily die in our jacuzzi.

Billy Me too. I love that jet stream. My crack's singin' hallelujah.

Lou So is mine.

She smiles. Pause. Billy grins. Pause.

Billy And the streets, the fuckin' streets out there, pristine, clean. Puts London to shame. You don't realise until you get away. London's fuckin' disgustin'. Dirt and filth. Litter, litter everywhere. Kids, that is. Fuckin' kids. It never used to be like that. Parents, that is. Fuckin' parents. We never used to drop litter. We did a lot of things, but we never fuckin' dropped litter.

Lou laughs.

What?

Lou You've turned into your dad.

Beat.

Billy Oh fuck, don't. That really would be frightenin'. But it's true, innit? I mean, here, here you could eat off the fuckin' sidewalk.

Lou I love the energy.

Billy The buzz, yeah, the buzz. Great, innit? The epicentre of the appetite that's eatin' the fuckin' planet. But there's somethin' about it that really suits me. It's kind of life-affirming.

Lou Shall we stay on a bit? Use the cards?

Beat.

Billy I'd love to.

Lou Let's do it, then.

Billy D'you know what? I could see myself never goin' back, I could. I mean, if things, if they went really well, and they loved us. I mean, you know, it could happen, it's a catchy tune, it could take off. And here's where the advert's on. This is where we should be. We should be here, ready to take advantage.

Lou I'm not goin' back to Derek, anyway. Whatever, I'm leavin' him. The marriage is over as far as I'm concerned.

   Pause.

Billy I hope you ain't leavin' him for me? (*Pause.*) Don't fuckin' leave him for me. It's nothin' to do with me, you and him. You leave him, that's up to you. But don't leave him for me. You ain't goin' from him to me. I ain't a marriage fuckin' breaker. I ain't the other fuckin' man. You're with someone, it's between you and them. You sort that out first. You leave, you're on your own. Then you're free to do what you fuckin' want. I don't want you. This is a mistake. This is a fuckin' mistake. It shouldn't have happened. It's wrong. You're a nightmare. It's over. Fuckin' nightmare, you. Me and you, fuckin' nightmare. Poison. You left me for dead. It's a miracle I'm fuckin' here. Bad news. Me and you, bad fuckin' news. It's over. Forget it. You're my worst fuckin' nightmare.

   Pause. Marc enters with a Freedom Card carrier bag.

Marc Ooh, shopping. You capitalist bastards. (*Sits.*) I met a right sort last night, I did. A bird from the Freedom Company. I firmed up the special relationship over a carrot in a vegan place. Inflatable tits. I'm in love. Yes please. I'll poodle her bush any day of the week. She thinks I'm Scottish. Och aye the noo. I'll take her up the high road, given half a chance.

John enters, absolutely rat-arsed.

John Ain't this great, eh? Ain't, ain't, ain't this fuckin' great? It's great. I fuckin', I fuckin', I fuckin' love America, I do. Friendly? Friendly? Fuckin' 'ell, friendly? I've had a great time, a great time, the bars, the people in bars, they put, they put fuckin' Harlesden to shame, they do. They do. I got some coke. D'you want some coke? I got some coke. Nice fella, lovely fella, fuckin' expensive though. But that's, that's the fuckin' exchange rate, innit. Good gear, fuckin' good gear, great gear. Great for drinkin'. Fantastic with a drink.

Marc Right. Coffee. I knew I should've kept an eye on you.

John What?

Marc She'll be here in a minute. Tuck your shirt in. Sit down. Don't say a word.

John What's up?

Marc You're pissed out of your brains. We've got a gig in seven hours.

John What's his problem? What's his fuckin' problem?

Marc Look, just sit down, you can sleep it off this afternoon.

John You what? You fuck? Don't fuckin' tell me.

Lou It's alright, John, sit down.

John Don't, don't fuckin' take sides with him, Lou. Don't, don't.

Billy Oi. Don't have a go at her.

John You. You. You fuckin' shut up too. You. I'll have your fuckin' eyes, eyes out.

39

*Gina, thirties, American, wearing a Freedom Card
T-shirt, enters and hovers on the periphery.*

Lou That's enough, John!

Billy Come on then. Come on.

Marc Leave it!

John Come on, you fuck!

Marc Behave.

He grabs John by the collar.

Billy Any time! Any time!

Gina Excuse me.

John You're dead! Fuckin' dead!

Marc pushes John onto a seat.

Gina Excuse me!

They all look over. Beat.

Marc Hello, babe, sorry about all this. They ain't house
trained. This is Gina, everyone.

Lou Hi, Gina.

Gina Hello.

Marc Billy.

Billy Alright?

Marc Not a pleasant sight. That's John. He's an animal,
don't worry . . .

John Oi. You. Fuck.

*Marc pushes him back down again and holds him
there with one hand.*

Marc It's alright, I've got his leash back in the room.

Gina Good. Welcome to America.

Billy I would feel welcome, but I've got a problem, actually. You've stuck us in a double room, we ain't a couple. And it's on the fourteenth floor, I've got a dodgy lung, so stairs are out, and I don't do lifts, I freak out in boxes. Can you sort me one out nearer ground zero, please?

John And my, my fuckin' mini-bar's shite.

Marc Shut up.

John It is. It's full of fuckin' water. Two bottles of Bud, a mini-scotch, and six, six bottles of fuckin' water. A bit of fuckin' bourbon, bourbon wouldn't go amiss.

Gina Anything else? Ho's? Drugs? Face-lifts?

Marc No. Sorry. Forget them. We are more than satisfied.

Gina Because Houston, we have a problem.

Marc Problem?

Gina The song.

Marc The song?

Gina 'Plastic People'.

Marc What about it?

Gina It sucks.

Marc What? What d'you mean?

Gina I mean it's risible, nauseous, an affront to humanity.

Marc I don't understand. I thought you loved it.

Gina The chorus. We love the chorus. It could've been written for us. I mean, that's all we needed to hear, so that's all we listened to. Thank God you gave me the CD last night. I took it to the gym this morning and nearly fell off the high-stepper. I called an emergency board meeting, and at nine a.m. we all listened to it.

Billy I'd love to have been a fly on that wall.

Gina The CEO nearly had a heart attack. I thought I'd have to give him mouth-to-dick resuscitation. I'm talking about one of the most powerful men in America. This guy's so rich he doesn't even have to work out. And I'm here to tell you, Billy. He hates Communists.

Billy I ain't a Communist, darlin'. I'm against all systems.

Gina Whatever.

Marc Hold up. What are you saying? You're still gonna use it for the ad, ain't you?

Gina As I said, the chorus is perfect. Until you put it with the other verses. Then it becomes kind of warped.

Billy Thank you. D'you want my autograph?

Marc I see where she's coming from. I take your point. It was written for another era. The world was a different place then.

Gina You can't sing those words at the launch.

Marc What you sayin'? The gig's cancelled?

Gina Absolutely not. My near-perfect two-thousand-dollar ass is on the line over this. And when my butt's threatened I step up to the plate.

She takes four sheets of paper from her briefcase.

I've had the creatives on it. These individuals are the *crème de la crème*. They're responsible for some of the greatest copy in history. From 'Just Do It' to 'Finger Lickin' Good'. And what they've come up with is a horse's ass, but that's cocaine for you. And it's better than the original. Not that that would take a genius.

She hands each of them a sheet of paper.

Tonight, for the launch, you're singing our version of the song.

Billy Is this a joke?

Gina If you wanna get paid, you'll do it.

Billy We've got a contract, darlin'. We're here, we're ready to fulfil our part, as stipulated. You wanna change the terms and conditions, tough shit.

Gina How quaint. A union man from the Jurassic period.

Billy You don't pay up and we'll see you in court.

Gina Let's cut to the chase. That old man is jumpin'. And with his fat ass, when he jumps it hits ten on the Richter scale. You don't play ball and he'll have you off the entire campaign.

Billy Fuck him. We'll see him in court.

Marc Hold on. I think we might need a bit of a band confab, Gina.

Billy Confab? What for? You can't seriously be considerin' this?

Marc Let's just calm down and have a look at the lyrics. We don't know what we're dealin' with yet.

Billy We're dealin' with the corporate American jackboot, that's what we're dealin' with! The squashin' of our culture! Taking something that means something, that has resonance, and puttin' it through the wringer so it comes out the other side as a dollar bill! The answer's no! You can fuck off!

Gina Lighten up, Billy. Your frown lines are freakin' me out.

Marc puts his arm around Gina and ushers her away.

Marc Give us ten minutes, babe. I'm sure we can sort something out.

Gina I'll be in the lobby.

She leaves.

Billy Look! Look at it! They've turned it into an advertisin' jingle!

Marc Let's just all take a deep breath and see what we're dealin' with.

They all read the new lyrics.

Billy
'I wanna set people free
Fulfil their destiny
Helped by the Freedom Company.'

John It, it scans well.

Billy Scans? Oh yeah, it scans! They've turned it into Beanz Meanz fuckin' Heinz!

Marc I know it brings up a credibility issue.

Billy Credibility? (*Laughs.*)

Marc But we're here now. It's twenty grand for five minutes' work. And we have to keep 'em sweet. We can't chance losin' the ad. No one'll know about it. There's a few hundred suits out there. I say we swallow it tonight. Keep our eyes on the prize.

John Yeah, yeah, he's right, he's right. You're right. Sorry, sorry about that earlier, Marc. Sorry. The click. The fuckin' click went. Sorry.

Billy This would be total fuckin' humiliation.

Marc Well, don't do it then. I'll do it. You'll still get your money. I'll humiliate myself on your behalf. There's no point discussin' it further. We know where we are. Let's just have a vote. I'm in. (*Raises his hand.*)

John Me too. I've, I've gotta think about my fuckin' mum.

Billy Well, I'm out. Lou?

Pause. Lou raises her hand. Billy storms off. Pause.

Marc Good riddance. Twat. Gnashin' and gnarlin' at our age, it's pathetic. We're doin' somethin' else now. We're tryin' to get on the rose-tinted bandwagon. That's the market we're lookin' at. Cuddly punks. That's what we've gotta be now if we're gonna get anywhere. Oh yeah, while I remember.

He takes two black turtle-neck sweaters with 'Freedom Card' emblazoned on back and front from the carrier bag and hands one each to the others.

They want us wearing these for the duration. We're company representatives.

John Turtle, turtle fuckin' necks. Sorry, sorry, no fuckin' way. I'll wear a stupid grin. I'll sing a fuckin', a fuckin' nursery rhyme. But that is my line in the sand. I won't wear a turtle fuckin' neck.

Marc Shut up and put it on.

John That, that's what I call fuckin' humiliation.

Marc Right, how am I gonna learn this shit? We'll need to rehearse. I'll see if we can get some extra time at the sound check. You, get some coffee down you.

John It's alright, it's alright. I've got some fuckin' coke.

Marc Give it here.

John What? No. I fuckin', I fuckin' need it. Sobers me up.

Marc Give it here. I need it. Front man? I'll show you two what a real front man is. Give me that fuckin' charlie. We'll see who's got charisma. Come on, give it me.

Billy enters.

Billy I've changed my mind. I'll do it.

Marc You'll do it?

Billy You heard, I'm in.

John That's brilliant. Thank, thank fuck for that.

Billy I've already sold my soul. I'm fuckin' Mephistopheles. I might as well get me just deserts. I crossed the line when I signed up. I mean, this is the logical fuckin' conclusion to that act, ain't it? It's the bald truth. In fact, you know what, it's fuckin' brilliant. 'Cos we won't be goin' out there pretending we're artists who haven't sold out, whose work is bein' subliminally fuckin' used to seduce people into buying things they don't want, as if it's nothing to do with them. We'll be saying, 'We're in sales now. Trust us. Spend, spend, spend.' It's the fuckin' truth. And I've always believed in tellin' the truth. So let's go out there like Cheshire cats and sell, sell, fuckin' sell.

Blackout.

SCENE SIX

A stage. The Freedom Card logo is projected onto a backdrop. The band are wearing Freedom Card turtle-necks. Billy, draped in the Stars and Stripes, microphone in hand, smiling manically at the audience, dementedly struts his stuff before launching into the song.

Billy

Wanna buy a house and a new TV
Sit and watch people I wanna be
I wanna buy a Rolex and a nice new car
Get behind the wheel and feel like a star
I wanna buy a washing machine
To keep my image clean
I wanna buy all I see
Helped by the Freedom Company
Plastic sets me free
Yeah plastic sets me free.

Wanna spend on a date
Meet my perfect mate
Then she'll become my wife
We'll have a romantic life
I wanna buy us some fun
Have a holiday in the sun
Let the little ones run
We'll be a happy family
With our new house and TV
Helped by the Freedom Company
Plastic sets us free
Yeah plastic sets us free.

All

Plastic people living in a plastic world
Plastic people looking really well
Life's so swell for plastic boys and girls
Because they're living in a plastic world
Living in a plastic world
Yeah they're living in a plastic world.

Billy

Wanna give to charity
Buy peace and prosperity
I wanna set people free
To be who they can be

Fulfil their destiny
Fucked by the Freedom Company.

Billy pulls out a knife, rips into the Stars and Stripes and screams.

Billy Fuck America! Fuck Freedom Cards!

Billy slits a wrist.

Lou No Billy!

Billy slits his other wrist.

Billy One point two million murders in fuckin' Iraq!

He plunges the knife into his stomach and falls to his knees.

Three cheers for Bin Laden!

Blackout.

SCENE SEVEN

A jail cell. New York. Marc and John.

John *Déjà vu*, this, innit, *déjà vu*. Oldham nick, Oldham, that was the last time we shared a cell.

Marc Harlow was the last cell we shared. Oldham was the second last.

John Harlow? Were we banged up in Harlow?

Marc The 'Fuck the Silver Jubilee' gig. When the National Front turned up.

John Oh yeah. Thank, thank God for the police, that night.

Marc We would've been dead without 'em.

John Kicked, kicked the fuckin' shit out of us. But at least, at least they saved us from the NF.

Marc That was his fault too. In walked the skins, and instead of calmin' it down, what's he do? He pulls a Union Jack down and has a piss on it. Psychotic twat.

John But that's what made him electric, bein' psychotic. If he weren't psychotic he wouldn't've been fuckin' magnetic.

Marc Watford. The Harrow Teds. That was another time he nearly got me killed. His fuckin' Elvis tribute.

John Oh fuck, yeah. 'The fat fuck died on the shitter.' Classic, fuckin' classic.

Marc I nearly lost my eye that night. My head was a fuckin' football. Brothel-creepers versus winkle-pickers. And he slipped out unharmed. I never noticed him helpin' me out. And that was just after I'd saved his life in fuckin' Croydon.

John Croydon? Oh yeah. Yeah, green grollies, Croydon. Synonymous, fuckin' synonymous. I went on with an umbrella that night. I had to throw it away the next day. I couldn't, I couldn't close the fuckin' thing, congealed, fuckin' congealed.

Marc He opens his mouth to start singin' and a beauty flies straight in.

John Beauty, fuckin' beauty.

Marc He goes berserk.

John Bottles, fuckin' glasses flyin'.

Marc This geezer has him pinned down and he's jabbin' his face with a broken bottle. I fuckin' kicked the shit out of the cunt and dragged Billy free. I saved his life about five times. What a cunt I am. What a fuckin' idiot.

John Well, I wouldn't be surprised if he's dead now.

Marc Here's hopin'.

John Limp, limp, a fuckin', a rag doll.

Marc I should've finished him off in Copenhagen.

John It wasn't through lack of tryin'.

Marc He's bleedin' to death and I put enough smack into the cunt to kill an elephant. He's like the geezer in *Halloween*, the bogeyman. You'd have to drive a stake through his heart and drown him in holy water to finish him off. And if I ever get the chance again I fuckin' well will.

John I keep, I keep forgettin' I weren't there. I keep nearly bringin' it up.

Marc Bring what up? You weren't there.

John I know, I know. That's why I keep rememberin' it.

Marc Rememberin' what?

Pause.

John Nothin'. I wasn't there.

Marc Ten out of ten. (*Pause.*) Get me out of here! Please, fuckin' please God. Oh God, please, please get me out of here. Please God. I swear, God. I give you my fuckin' word. I swear on my dog's life. Get me home safe and sound and I promise. Cross my heart. On my life. I mean it. I will give up the music biz. Help me to give it up. Please help me to give it up.

John I think, I think he might've already answered your call on that one.

Marc Maybe he has. Maybe that's the one good thing that's gonna come out of this. If this has finally put an end to that road, thank you, God, for saving me from my grovelling desperation. My mental illness that is the music fuckin' biz. Thirty years of living for the dream that someday I'd be a successful vinyl battery hen for CBS or EMI. And why? Why? D'you know why I came into the music fuckin' biz? D'you know what drove my ambition?

John Stardom?

Marc My dick.

John Oh yeah, course, yeah. What else is there, really?

Marc Birds and my dick brought me into this God-forsaken business. All I really wanted was to get my dick sucked.

John Well, you certainly got that out of it.

Marc I should've been born with a fanny.

John That, that would've been fuckin' interestin'.

Marc My big dick has fucked up my life.

John My fuckin', my fuckin' little dick's fucked up mine.

Marc It's never been able to settle down, even when it was in love. Whatever that means.

John I was gonna say, what, what happened with Caz?

Marc Don't. That was a ding-dong. She was the best ding-dong I ever had. She had me sorted. She believed in me. Never wavered. When The Turds folded, there she was, pickin' up the pieces and turnin' me into a New Romantic. The Dandy's.

John The Dandy's. You were fuckin' great, you were. I thought you were gonna make it.

Marc We nearly did. She got us on *New Faces*. Mickey Most thought we had somethin'. But we got beaten into second place by a dog that was a trapeze artist.

John Yeah, I saw it, actually. I fuckin', I fuckin' voted for you. But the pooch, the pooch was fuckin' special.

Marc When that went kaput, she turned me into Robbie Robot. I was like a kind of Gary Numan type. It nearly fuckin' happened. I was on the cusp as Robbie. She knocked down the doors at EMI and got me a fuckin' recordin' contract. But it didn't work out. I was on the floor again. She picked me up, dusted me down, and turned me into a disco king, Marvin Goldust again, she was like a dog with a bone, out there, pushin' for me, until, er . . . until she walked in on me bangin' a charlady. End of. She gave me confidence, see. I've got no confidence. I don't realise how good I am. I'm frightened, John. I'm scared I'll die alone. A failure. Just me and my cock. Earth to earth. Ashes to ashes. RIP. Marc Faeces. 'He could have been big if he didn't have a cock.'

Billy (*off*) Fuck off! I am a British citizen! Aaagh! Police brutality! I demand to see the British Ambassador! Get off me! Cunts! You fuckers! Aaagh!

The cell door opens. Billy, bandaged up, black eye, bloodstained Freedom Card T-shirt, is pushed in and falls to the floor.

Aaagh!

The cell door is shut and locked. Pause. Billy gives Marc and John a cursory glance before dragging himself, in obvious pain, across the floor to rest against a wall.

John I'm amazed they let you out of hospital so quick.

Billy The medical insurance don't cover suicide attempts.

Marc No? What an oversight. I must make sure we get that the next time.

Billy There won't be a next time.

Marc You can be certain of that.

Billy Wankers! They fuckin' overreact to everythin'.
A few words and a bit of blood – mine – and they throw
the fuckin' Patriot Act at us. Tossers.

Marc The what?

Billy The Patriot Act. Defacing the American flag.
Incitin' terrorism.

Marc Are you fuckin' serious?

Billy It's bullshit. They're just tryin' to frighten us.

Marc I hope you fuckin' told 'em that we knew nothing?
You acted totally alone?

Billy All I've said is 'No comment.'

Marc This could be really fuckin' serious. They could
lock us all up for fuckin' years!

Billy I don't recognise the court. I'll refuse to give it
legitimacy. I'll fuckin' quote Saddam Hussein as my legal
precedent.

*Marc jumps on Billy and starts to throttle him. Billy
goes puce.*

John Marc. (*Beat.*) Marc! (*Beat.*) Marc!

*John tries to pull Marc off. Marc continues to throttle
Billy, who has stopped struggling.*

Marc!

Marc lets Billy go. He falls to the floor, gasping for air.

Marc The day that little arsehole knocked on my door
was the worst day of my life.

Billy It was the best day of mine.

Marc You had greasy long hair and a plum in your mouth.
Like the middle-class student you were.

Billy We all come from somewhere.

Marc You sang fuckin' 'Stairway to Heaven'. Led fuckin' Zeppelin. And you sang it in tune. I was quite impressed. Then when I said you weren't what I was lookin' for your lip went. Like a fuckin' *Pop Idol* wannabe in front of Simon Cowell.

Billy The Gorilla.

Marc You even said those classic words, 'This means more to me than anything in the world. You're wrong. I'm gonna to be a star.' I said, 'Sorry, mate, I'm lookin' for an anti-star.' 'A what?' Derr. 'Go and see The Sex Pistols.' 'The what?' I should've kept me mouth shut. A week later you turned up with spiky green hair and the beginnings of a Dick Van Dyke cockney accent.

Billy 'Chim chiminee chim chiminee chim chim cheree.'

Marc I knew, I fuckin' knew you had a screw loose. But I was lookin' for a fuckin' lunatic, so you were in.

Billy It was a nice asylum run by a cunt.

Marc Over the next month you developed a phlegm problem, a sulfate habit, and a fuckin' hunchback.

John The bells, the fuckin' bells.

Marc Tony Parsons got you spot on in the *NME*. 'Billy Abortion is a cartoon punk. A third-rate Johnny Rotten clone.'

Billy Was that the same article where he called you a 'cut-price burlesque queen'.

Marc Only because you weren't Rotten. You weren't the real McCoy. You had to outdo him to prove yourself. If he wanted to offend, you wanted to abuse. He spat on stage so you had to throw up. When he wrote 'God Save the Queen', you responded with that classic, 'Shoot the Royal Bitch'.

Billy Which you refused to play because you didn't want to upset your mummy.

Marc And then when Sid joined 'em and took bein' a wanker to another level, you thought you had to outdo him. He got into smack, so you got into smack.

Billy I was into smack before him. I had my first hit with 'Johnny Thunders' when he first came over. Sid followed me. I was one of the first Brit punks into smack.

Marc How proud you must be.

Billy I'm just putting you right on the chronology.

Marc And when Sid and Nancy copped it, you tried to force Lou down that road.

Billy It was her who stabbed me. Not the other way round.

Marc You had her pinned down. You were tryin' to jack her up.

Billy She wanted it.

Marc Bollocks.

Billy A 'no' was a 'yes' from her lips. That was our game. We role-reversed sometimes. She did it for me. I did it for her.

Marc She was pregnant with your baby, you cunt! She miscarried on my kitchen floor when we got back to London.

Pause.

Billy That's bullshit.

Marc He was there, ask him.

Billy looks to John.

John I, I, I fuckin' cleaned it up. I, I fuckin' flushed it down the toilet.

Pause.

Marc She dumped you, didn't she? She was packed and ready to leave and you, with your warped fuckin' mind, you thought you could keep hold of her by jackin' her up.

Billy She said nothin' about a baby.

Marc To you? You were so far gone she knew she had to get away for the sake of the fuckin' baby. You'd become the classic music business fuckin' victim. You started out not knowing who you were, and wanting to be someone you weren't. You found a role model, twisted it a bit, struck a pose, and, lo and behold, Cliff to Elvis, it worked. A little bit of success, a lot of attention, a few hero-worshipping fans, an expanding ego, and, hey presto, there you go, Billy Abortion, a cartoon version of someone else's fuckin' image. You swallowed the whole bullshit kaboodle and headed down that well-worn rock 'n' roll track of sex, drugs, and fuckin' death. The only pity is, you never quite had the bottle to fulfil your plastic fuckin' destiny. You could never go that extra inch and actually top yourself, you fuckin' poser. The next time you feel like havin' a go, give me a call, I'll come over with a rope and kick the fuckin' chair away.

The jail door is unlocked and opened. Gina enters.

Marc Hello, babe. I'm so, so sorry.

Gina So am I.

Marc We really did have nothin' to do with it.

Gina You're free to go.

Marc Really?

Gina If I were you I'd get out of here before they change their minds.

John Yeah, yeah, come on. Let's go.

Marc I hope it's not been too detrimental to the launch.

Gina There was no launch. Tonight never happened.

Marc Oh, right. Well that suits us. We were never here.

Gina We've pulled the commercial.

Marc You've pulled it?

Gina We've put it on hold for a month. We'll relaunch then.

Marc Oh right. Good.

Gina You're off the soundtrack.

Marc Oh no.

Gina Well, what did you expect?

Marc Now hold on. Wait. Listen. I'll re-record the soundtrack. We'll get rid of him. We'll make a statement, 'We deplore his actions. It was nothin' to do with us. He's sacked from the band.' We'll wave American flags. Whatever you want. You tell us. We'll do it.

Gina It's too late, Marc. Another song's already being lined up. They're replacing 'Plastic People' with 'Freedom', by Sir Paul McCartney. The song he wrote in response to 9/11.

Billy 11/9.

Gina What?

Billy Nothing.

Gina A very dear friend of mine died on 9/11.

57

Billy A very dear friend of mine died on 24/6.

Gina What happened to you as a child, Billy? Was your father a paedophile?

Billy No, worse than that. He was a bank manager.

Gina Only you've got the emotional development of a two-year-old, trapped inside the body of a decomposing corpse. Hate, Billy, deal with it. It's no good for wrinkles. Get some therapy.

Billy I think I'll try botox instead.

Gina The amount of botulism you'd need to iron out that dried prune you call a face would be enough to wipe out Asia.

Billy I'll come back here. Release it in New York.

Gina The only thing you need to release is your poor pus-filled tortured soul. I bet you wake up every morning and think, 'I hate myself, I hate this life, I hate this world, it stinks.'

Billy Have we slept together?

Gina I may have screwed way too many deadbeats, baby, but I draw the line at necrophilia.

She heads for the door again.

Marc Hold on. There must be somethin' we can do? Come on, babe. I'm on my knees. We'll do anythin'.

She turns.

Gina Take it up with the board. I've been fired. Thanks, guys.

Marc Whoa, wait, that's out of order, that is. You should sue. We'll make statements. We'll back you up. I'll tell you what, we'll back you up, and you back us up. We'll sue too. Our contract's signed. Tonight's debacle was totally separate from the advert agreement. We should launch some kind of joint action.

Gina The fat man's sung, guys.

Marc I'm not lettin' you take this lying down. We can help each other out here. You shouldn't give up that easy.

Gina Give up? *Moi*? Let me tell you how it goes. *Mañana*, I'll wake up with a hangover, no job, and feeling like a sack of shit. You know what I'll do? Here's a tip for you, Billy. I'll jump in the shower, think about that. I'll spend twenty minutes exfoliating with seaweed and bran body soufflé. Fifteen minutes lathering myself with luxury vitamin E body wash. Then I'll raise my soon-to-be-moisturised arms, open my lungs, and belt out Gloria Gaynor's 'I Will Survive' until I believe it. Twenty minutes' meditation, and my heart will open and divine light will flood in. I'll throw in a couple of affirmations, 'I will prevail. Today's gonna be a great day. I will prevail.' By the time I walk out of that apartment in my fuck-me Jimmy Choos, and my don't-fuck-with-me Donna Karan, I'll be so hot, Wall Street'll melt in front of my pussy. Positive energy, Billy. The American way, baby. Try it.

She leaves. Blackout.

SCENE EIGHT

Heathrow Airport. Baggage reclaim. John, pissed, enters, pushing a trolley loaded with Billy and their luggage. He rams it into a wall.

Billy Aagh!

John (*in Billy's face*) Sorry.

Pause. He backs off, deliberately knocking Billy's arm in the process.

Billy Aagh!

John Sorry.

John picks up a bottle of duty-free whisky from the trolley, opens it and raises it to toast.

Sid. (*Swigs.*) Fuckin', fuckin' Vicious, you cunt. Here's, here's to you.

He swigs and offers Billy the bottle.

Billy No thanks.

John You fuckin', fuckin' . . . Toast, toast the fuckin' man. He's floatin', floatin' around here.

Billy What?

John You fuckin' what? Call yourself a punk, a fuckin' punk? He's here. He's in the fuckin', the fuckin' air conditionin'. Show some fuckin' respect.

Billy What you talkin' about?

John Sid. Sid the fuckin' Vicious. His ashes. His fuckin' particles. They're fuckin' waftin', waftin' around the air conditionin' here.

Billy Don't bother with the punch line.

John Punch line? Punch line? I'll fuckin' punch. Punch. His urn, his urn got smashed when they brought him back from New York! In fuckin', in fuckin' cargo. Alright? Alright? His ashes, ashes, fuckin' sucked up. He's forever, forever fuckin' condemned to be floatin' around the back passages, the fuckin' back passages of fuckin' Heathrow. Punch line? Fuck. Punch line? Now fuckin' toast him.

Pause. Billy takes the bottle.

Billy How very apt. (*Toasts.*) Sid. That's karma, mate. That's fuckin' karma. (*Swigs.*)

Marc enters, listening to his mobile.

Marc Nightmare! It's a fuckin' nightmare! Someone video'd the whole thing. It was on last night's news. Sky have been showin' your *hara-kiri* attempt in slow fuckin' motion.

Lou enters, listening to her mobile.

Lou We're front page in all the tabloids!

Marc The *Sun* are on my voicemail. 'What did we think of the London bombings? Did we support them? Is there any reason why we shouldn't be charged with incitement to terrorism?'

Lou The *Mail*. The *Daily Mail*! Shhh! . . . Oh no.

John What?

Lou They know you've been workin' as a session musician while the dole paid your mortgage, Marc.

Marc What?

Lou They've informed the Inland Revenue.

Marc You shit!

He kicks Billy.

Billy Aaagh!

John Shut up!

He punches Billy.

Billy Ow!

Marc Shhh! The *Star*. The *Star*.

John The *Star*? That's my paper. The *Star*.

Marc Have you had a boob job, Lou?

Lou What?

Marc Have you had a boob job? They seem to think you've had a job on your tits.

Lou I've had a cancerous one removed. If that's what they mean.

Marc Would you be interested in a photo shoot?

Lou The *Guardian*! Oh my God! The fuckin' *Guardian*!

John The *Guardian*? Fuckin' 'ell. The *Guardian*. This is fuckin' mega.

Lou They want to do a feature on us.

John A feature? A feature in the *Guardian*?

Lou They want to talk to us about artistic integrity.

John Artistic integrity? The *Guardian*. The *Guardian*. Artistic fuckin', fuckin' integrity. I wish my old man was still alive. I wish. That would've shut, shut the cunt up. Artistic integrity and me in the fuckin' *Guardian*.

Marc Respect? What the fuck's that? Respect? Would we be interested in performing at a benefit for the Stop the War Coalition?

John Stop the war? Fuck. Stop the war! Yeah, I'm in, I'm in. What war?

Marc Oh my God. There's someone from Al Jazeera with 'em.

John Al Jazeera? Fuck me. Al Jazeera.

Marc Their London correspondent. Can he interview us?

John That makes sense. They, they fuckin' love suicides on that channel.

Lou The *Mirror*. The *Mirror*.

John The *Mirror*. The fuckin' *Mirror*. We're famous again. We're fuckin' famous.

Billy It's better than that. We're infamous again.

John Infamous. Yeah, fuckin' infamous. We're fuckin' infamous again.

Lou I'm really sorry, John.

John What?

Pause.

Lou Your mum's dead. (*Pause.*) They're saying you receive a carer's allowance to look after her. But you left her alone for the weekend when she was incapable of lookin' after herself.

John My sister was goin' to pop in three times a day.

Lou I'm so sorry.

Marc The *Sun* again. You, Billy. Your ex-wife. She . . . She's shocked, apparently. She reckons you wouldn't say boo to a goose. And your ex-boss at IBM. He says you were a model employee. Twenty years' service without a word of complaint. Apparently no one's seen you since you cracked up when your wife ran off with the milkman. Any comments?

Pause. Hundreds of camera flashes. They all face front. Freeze-frame with them all giving various finger and hand gestures.

All Wankers.

Camera flashes. Another freeze-frame.

Billy Rupert Murdoch's a paedophile! He's bought himself a Thai bride!

Camera flashes. Another freeze-frame.

Marc We're artists with integrity! We ain't for sale! You can't buy us!

Camera flashes. Another freeze-frame. Lou is about to open her blouse.

Lou D'you wanna see a bird who's had a tit lopped off?

Camera flashes. Another freeze-frame. Billy shows his arse.

John We, we, we are The Dysfunckshonalz. And we've got nothin', nothin', nothin' to fuckin' say!

Marc Downloads available at www. the dysfunckshonalz. co.uk.

All Bollocks!

SCENE NINE

Marc's flat. The early hours of the morning. The drink has flowed and the band are well-oiled. All have beers on the go. Marc and John stare at the computer which is connected to their website. Lou sits quietly in a corner, relentlessly downing a bottle of vodka. Billy stares out through a gap in the curtains.

Billy Scumbags. The flotsam and fuckin' jetsam. (*He opens the curtains and gesticulates.*) Here I am, boys! Teeth and fuckin' smiles.

Camera flashes from outside. John and Marc run to join Billy and gesticulate.

Marc Wankers!

John Wankers!

More camera flashes.

Billy All publicity's good publicity.

John Wank, wank, wankers.

Billy The symbiotic relationship. (*Closes curtains.*)

Marc We've gotta keep this goin'.

Billy No kids gone missin' at the moment, are there? No distraught parents to deify, then fuckin' crucify? No new Jack the Rippers killin' prostitutes? Fuck me, we're in luck, lads, they need us to be offensive. Help 'em to sell a few fuckin' papers.

John Offensive. Offensive. We can be fuckin' offensive. We were one of the most offensive, offensive bands in fuckin' history.

Marc 'Jesus Was a Wanker'. B side. 'Jesus Was a Wanker'.

John Fuck, fuck, yeah, fuckin' 'ell.

Marc *and* **John** (*sing*)
Jesus was a wanker
Priests are all perverts
Jesus was a wanker
'Cos he loved it when it hurt.

John That's, that's stood the test of fuckin' time. That's as offensive, fuckin' offensive now as it was then.

Billy No it ain't. The world's moved on since then. You been in a fuckin' coma?

Marc Yeah, he's right. Havin' a pop at Christians is fuckin' *passé*.

Billy Oxygen. Fan the flames. Think, boys. Use your grey matter.

John Fuck. Fuck this. Alright. Got it, fuckin' swap, swap fuckin' Jesus, yeah. Swap him for you know, fuckin', fuckin', what's his name, the geezer with the funny, funny fuckin' hat.

Beat.

Billy Tommy Cooper?

John No, fuckin', you know . . .

Marc I know. And no. No way, you dick. I wanna live to enjoy the fruits. I don't want a fuckin' *fatwah* on me.

John A fat what?

Marc Don't even go there. Shut it. Someone might hear.

Billy (*looking at the computer screen*) Get ready to celebrate. We're on 999.

John Fuck me. Fuck me.

Marc We're usually lucky to get three or four downloads a year. This is it. It's happenin'.

John Ballistic. We're fuckin' goin' ballistic.

Billy First thing tomorrow we'll have to sign up with iTunes.

Marc Now you're talkin' my language.

Billy If you can't beat 'em –

Marc Download charts, here we come.

Billy Here we go. One thousand.

Marc goes for a celebratory jump around the room and chants.

Marc One thousand, one thousand, one thousand.

John joins the celebratory dance.

Both One thousand, one thousand, one thousand. One thousand, one thousand, one thousand.

Marc We are back. Bring on the Stop the fuckin' War gig.

Billy We ain't doin' that.

Marc What? Why not? What's wrong with doin' that? That's our market. That's what you've tapped us into. The anti-Yank market.

John We could go fuckin' platinum, platinum in that market.

Billy We've had an email. There's a punk reunion gig at the Shepherds Bush Empire next week. The UK Subs have dropped out and they wants us to replace 'em. Second on the bill.

John Second, second?

Billy Above The Vibrators and beneath The Damned.

John Fuckin' 'ell. Above The Vibrators! Fuck me!

Marc That's fuckin' brilliant.

Billy And you know what we open with? 'Suicidal Tendencies'.

Marc 'Suicidal Tendencies'?

Billy We'll use the video footage of New York. We'll have it projected on a backdrop. Me stickin' the knife in overlaid with me singin' 'Suicidal Tendencies'.

Marc That's genius. That is marketing genius. (*Picks up an acoustic guitar.*) I can see it. Drums, come on, drums, I can see it.

> *John drums on the back of a chair. Marc plays the intro.*

Billy (*sings*)
Hate my fuckin' mum
I hate my fuckin' dad
I hate my fuckin' life
I think I'm goin' mad
The world is full of bullshit
The news is all crap
I don't want to be here but I haven't got a map.

Marc Slash one wrist.

Billy
So I slashed my wrists this morning

Marc Slash the other wrist.

Billy
Jumped in the river this afternoon

Marc *Hara-kiri*.

Billy
Tonight I'm gonna hang myself
Won't be a day too soon –

Marc Jump-cut *hara-kiri*.

Billy
Suicidal Tendencies are what I live for –

Marc More *hara-kiris*.

Billy
Suicidal Tendencies, without them life's a bore.

They applaud themselves.

John I'll tell you what, that fuckin', that fuckin' pisses on 'Bohemian, Bohemian fuckin' Rhapsody'.

Marc Fuck 'Bohemian Rhapsody'. That pisses on fuckin' 'Thriller'.

Billy It pisses on every phoney music video in history. It'll be the first reality music video.

John It was nearly the first fuckin' snuff, snuff music video.

Marc Would MTV show it, though? That's a consideration.

Billy Fuck them. We do it ourselves. Stick it on the web page. You mark my words, it's a sick world, we'll get more hits than Harry fuckin' Potter.

Marc I think you might be right.

Billy I know I'm right. There's a lot of warped and fucked-up people out there. That's our market. And I'll tell you what, it's a fuck of a sight bigger than the anti-American market.

Lou explodes, and throws the bottle of vodka against a wall. It smashes.

Lou You fucking wankers! Men! Fucking men! I hate 'em!

They all look over, shocked. Pause.

John What's, what's up, Lou?

Lou What's up? What's fucking up? A few hours ago you fucking hated him. Now you're both on your knees proclaiming him a genius! Happy, Billy? Happy now? You're the leader of the band again! You've got your acolytes back. A couple of decrepit, middle-aged, fuckin' retards.

John Oi! Oi!

Lou Congratulations!

Billy It ain't like that.

Marc Calm down, Lou.

Lou He's just cost you forty grand and you're sucking his cock!

Marc Whoa. Hold on. OK. Alright, so we've had differences. But we're here now, and this is a serious opportunity. If this takes off, forty grand could be peanuts.

Lou Take off? You lot? A bunch of grandad fucking wannabes! A shit group of has-beens that never really fuckin' were!

Marc Watch out, lads, she's back. The *Nightmare on Elm Street*'s resurfaced. I knew she was still in there somewhere.

Lou You're a fucking joke!

Marc Helmets on, boys. I think she's on, must be that time of the month. Remember the drill, lads. Lou's got PMT, batten down the hatches.

Pause.

John Fuck, fuck. I think you might've overstepped the mark there, Marc. The Hulk, The fuckin' Hulk's makin' a comeback. She's got, she's got her old Hulk face comin' on.

Pause.

Lou I haven't had a period since I aborted my beautiful little boy on your black-and-white kitchen lino.

Pause. She picks up her handbag and heads for the door.

Billy Lou . . .

Lou turns on him.

Lou Don't. I don't want to hear it. I fucking hate you. You're a fucking vampire. In those two miserable years you sucked me dry and turned me into a barren fucking shell. You literally sucked the fucking life out of me. And now, I can't believe I've let you fucking do it to me again. I must be mentally ill. I've had memory block. Why? Why the fuck did I want to spend the last few precious months of my life on this planet, with you?

Billy What?

Lou I'm going to die. I will be dead and buried very soon.

Billy But you . . .

Lou I lied. I lied because I wanted to have a great time. I was about to start another bout of chemo when I got the call from that walking fucking penis. I thought it was the voice of God. Don't wither away in a whimper. Go for it. Grab life. Relive that bright spot in the past. Have a laugh. Heal wounds. Go out with a bang. Instead . . . instead . . . I've found myself back in the nightmare it really fucking was.

Pause. She exits.

SCENE TEN

A dressing room in the Shepherds Bush Empire. Marc, punked up like a pantomime dame, waits like a cat on hot bricks. The door opens.

Marc Thank God for that. Thank you, God. I've been havin' kittens.

Billy and John enter, wearing funeral garb and carrying bags.

John Traffic.

Marc We're on in fuckin' fifteen.

Billy We'll be ready.

Marc When are either of you two gonna get a mobile? It's fuckin' Neanderthal. I've been coverin'. Everyone thinks you're here.

Billy We are here.

Marc I've had to put up with that cunt, Sensible. He can't wait to see you two. He couldn't wait to fuckin' rub it in. Soon as I got here, 'You seen the download charts?'

John What's happened?

Marc You don't know? I thought you would've checked 'em, first thing.

Billy We've been to a funeral.

Marc Oh yeah, I know, yeah, course, sorry. Alright, was it?

Billy We ain't in 'em. We dropped out.

John Shit.

Marc There's still fuckin' hope. If we can get a buzz goin' again, press are out there tonight. And listen to this. Are you listenin'? We've been offered a tour of northern Europe.

John Oh yes. Northern Europe. I'll have, have some of that.

Marc Good whack too. Ten grand.

John Ten grand, fuck. That'll, that'll do me.

Marc Split three ways. Minus whatever.

John When? When?

Marc Two weeks. They want to get us out there while the buzz is still goin'. The plan goes, Hamburg, Gothenburg, Reykjavik, Oslo, Helsinki, Copenhagen.

Billy Copenhagen?

Marc Yeah, well, I did say, I said, er, not sure about Copenhagen.

Billy I am. Fuck it. Why not?

Marc Oh good. Great. Bury the hatchet, yeah. So to speak. Not literally.

John Copenhagen. Norway, fuck Norway. Great.

Marc I'll see you out there. I'm goin' to psych up. Psych up. Psych up.

Marc leaves. The others take off their trousers. John's underpants are emblazoned with a swastika. They both take pairs of bondage trousers from their bags and put them on.

Billy I'm shittin' myself.

John Drink. Drink.

Billy Drink? I need a Mandrax.

John Attitude. Attitude. Remember, anyone that likes us is a fuckin' cunt.

Billy Mandrax is what got me through our first gig.

John Yeah, yeah. Staines. Staines fuckin' Civic Hall.

Billy . . . Borehamwood.

John Borehamwood?

Billy I walked onstage, the Mandrax kicked in, and magic. I knew, I thought, this is me, I want some of this. Three songs in, 'Suburban Nightmare', and the student union pulled the fuckin' plug.

John That's right, that's right. Greasy fuckin' long-haired cunt.

Billy That's when I knew we had somethin' special. When that hippy pulled the plug I knew we were goin' somewhere.

John I can see it now. Your fuckin' boot. His broken nose. That's im, imprinted on my brain.

Billy takes a straitjacket from his bag. John takes an old ripped and safety-pinned T-shirt from his. They put them on.

Billy It's too easy to forget the highs.

John Yeah, fuck, yeah. I can't remember fuck all, me. I went, I went to a party in 1976, and I left in 1989. All I can remember is a blur. I've got images, flashes. You, you in a Nazi uniform tryin' to get into Anne Frank's house. Lou, Lou fryin' one of your turds with onions, and tellin' Marc it was a steak sandwich. His face, his fuckin' face when you told him.

Billy Me bleedin' to death in Copenhagen?

Pause.

John What?

Billy Surely that's imprinted?

John What? Fuck off. I wasn't there.

Billy Yes, you were. I know you were. I was half comotose and you were runnin' around like a headless chicken. That image is indelibly fuckin' printed in my head.

John Is it? Fuck. I was there? Was I? No?

Billy You went through my pockets, stole my fags, and fucked off.

John Me? What? Fuck off.

Billy I'm just tellin' you. I know. I was barely conscious, but I know. Fasten me up, yeah.

John fastens Billy's straitjacket.

John I was there. But, but, what you don't know, what you don't fuckin' know is, I saved your fuckin' life.

Billy Fuck the bullshit.

John But it's true.

Billy It don't matter, I don't blame you, I'm just lettin' you know.

John On my life. I promise. I did, I saved your fuckin' life. Marc, Lou, they were in the lift, they were callin' a fuckin' cab. Me, me, I had to check, I couldn't believe you were fuckin' dead. I smacked your face, I pumped your fuckin' heart, I fuckin', I fuckin' gave you the fuckin', the kiss of fuckin' life. I fuckin' tongued you. Fuckin' 'ell, and then you like, spluttered. And I, oh fuck. I brought you back to life, nicked your fags and got out of there. It was me phoned the hotel from the airport. I told 'em, I fuckin' told 'em, your room needs servicin'. Gospel, gospel, fuckin' gospel. You fuckin' owe me. A greater, greater love hath, hath no fuckin' cunt. Stickin' my tongue down your fuckin' throat. I needed a fuckin' pack of fags after that. You can't, you can't fuckin' begrudge me ten Bensons after that. You owe me.

Billy I'll buy you a pint.

John A pint? A fuckin' pint? The Victoria, Victoria Cross. That's what I fuckin' deserve.

John takes his Cambridge Rapist mask from his bag and struggles to pull it on.

Torture, this is. Fuckin' torture.

A knock on the door.

Billy We're comin'.

75

The door opens and Lou pops her head in.

John Lou, fuckin' 'ell, Lou. Tell me you've come to play, fuckin' tell me.

Lou No way. I just wanted to say good luck. I'm out front.

John Shit. Shame. Fuck. You sure? You sure?

Lou I'm sure.

John Fuck. Walt Disney. I was lookin' for a Walt Disney moment. Shame.

Lou I'm sorry I couldn't make your mum's funeral.

John That's OK, don't –

Lou I had a hospital appointment this mornin', and –

John Honestly, no, fuck, it's just, er, I wish . . . I wish she could've fuckin' seen me tonight.

John breaks down and sobs. Lou puts her arms round him. Billy puts his head on his shoulder.

Billy No shame in emotion, mate. Let it go.

John Right. That's enough. OK. Let's go. See you out there. I'm suffocatin'. Jesus fuck, I'm suffo-fuckin'-catin'.

He leaves. Pause.

Lou I just wanted to say good luck.

She turns to leave.

Billy What's happenin' with the cancer?

She stops and turns. Pause.

Lou It's spread. It's got into my lymphs and . . . but it's gonna be alright. I start . . . I start the chemo again in a couple of weeks.

Billy A couple of weeks? What are they waitin' for?

Lou There's a waitin' list. But it's not long. It'll be okay. I feel like somethin's shifted, I really do. I'm gonna beat it. I just know I am. (*Pause.*) Anyway, get out there and give me a great night. That's what I'm here for. That's what I call medicine.

Pause.

Sorry.

Pause.

Lou Goodbye, Billy.

Long pause as they look at each other as if it's for the last time. She turns to go.

Billy Lou.

Lou stops. Beat. She turns to face him.

You're goin' private. No questions. Fuck the NHS. It's shit. You're goin' private. I'm payin'.

Lou Don't be stupid.

Billy That's what's happenin'.

Lou You ain't got no money.

Billy I have. I've got it comin'. Loads of it. I'm gonna be rich.

Beat. Marc enters, followed by John.

Marc Come on. They're screamin' for us. We're on.

Billy Come on with us, Lou. Fuck it. Come on. We'll find a bass, come on.

John Yeah, yeah. Come on, make my night, make my night, Lou.

Billy The four of us. One last time. You can't say no.

Lou Oh bollocks. OK.

John Yes! Yes! *Mary Poppins*! *Mary* fuckin' *Poppins*!

Marc But as long as you know you ain't on the tour. That's all organised for three. Accommodation, money. It's only worth it split three ways.

Billy I'm afraid I can't do the tour.

Marc What?

John Why? Why?

Billy I'll be in Australia.

Marc Australia?

John Australia?

Billy In the jungle.

Marc The jungle?

John The jungle? The jungle?

Billy I'm goin' on *I'm a Celebrity Get Me Out of Here!*

    Pause.

Marc You can't be fuckin' serious?

Billy I can't turn it down. They're givin' me fifty grand.

Marc When did this come up?

Billy A couple of days ago. I've been stewin' on it. But I've decided to go.

Marc What about us?

Billy Sorry.

Marc You cunt.

Billy I know. Sorry.

Pause.

Marc Fuck you. We don't need you anyway. We'll do it without you. I'll piss on you as a front man. We'll get a dummy in your place. 'I'll never sell out.' Wanker!

He leaves.

John I hope, I fuckin' hope they make you eat a kangaroo's fuckin' anus.

He leaves.

Lou I'm not havin' you sell out for me.

Billy Sell out? Bollocks. I'm cashin' in.

Lou But –

John No buts, babe. I'm doin' it.

Lou I won't let you sell your principles on my behalf.

Billy Fuck principles. It'll be a relief. I don't know what I believe any more, anyway. What used to be true probably fuckin' wasn't anyway. The truth? There's no such thing. It just depends on where you're standin'. And right now I'm standin' here with you. And I ain't lettin' you out of my fuckin' sight ever again. Come on. You're about to witness the extinction of a species. The last of the dinosaurs. I'm goin' under the hammer, babe. And I'm gonna squeeze it dry. So let the biddin' fuckin' begin.

He leaves. Beat. Lou follows.

SCENE ELEVEN

The stage at the Shepherds Bush Empire. The end of the set. Billy, at the microphone, looks out at the audience, and scans them.

Billy Look at the state of you lot. Well fed, nicely clothed, a few spangles. Come on, get your credit cards out. I wanna see 'em, all of 'em. Get 'em out. Let's wave 'em in the air. Fuck lighters. Let's do it with plastic.

He waits until satisfied with the response.

What a lovely sight, that is. I've got a message for you lot. No sell out! No surrender! I am the opposition! The world shouldn't be the way it is! Black should be white! White should be black! The poor should be rich! The rich should be poor!

He spreads his arms and his straitjacket opens.

Oh yes. That's better. That feels good. Ooh baby, baby. Insanity, here I come.

He takes the straitjacket off.

Free! Free! Free at fuckin' last! I'm joinin' the throng. I'm in. You've got me. I'm one of you cunts. I'm fuckin' plastic too. One, two, three, four . . .

He launches into the song. Gone is the sneering, malevolent, cynicism of his original performance. In its place is a straight-down-the-line, middle-of-the-road interpretation.

Wanna buy a house and a new TV
Sit and watch people I wanna be
I wanna buy a nice new car
Get behind the wheel and feel like a star
I wanna buy a washing machine

To keep my image clean
I wanna buy a brand new me
From a corporate company
Then I'll know how to be a pristine plastic me.

Wanna buy a personality
To present the plastic me
I wanna buy a plastic wife
Cut out the trouble and strife
I wanna buy us some fun
A holiday in the sun
Give her a plastic bun
We'll be a plastic family
With a new house and TV
And we'll sit and watch people we wanna be.

All
Plastic people living in a plastic world
Plastic people looking really well
Life's so swell for plastic boys and girls
Because they're living in a plastic world
Living in a plastic world
Yeah they're living in a plastic world.

Billy
Wanna buy a family car
The old one's for a star
I wanna buy a washing machine
The last one's a has-been
I wanna buy another me
Set the real one free
To pre-package himself
Be a product on a shelf
And then I'll consume myself
That way I'll increase my wealth
Destroy my mental health.

Marc You cunt!

Marc attacks Billy. A fight ensues. Lou tries to break it up. John joins the fray. It's a bundle. Lights fade. Police sirens and flashing lights. A sound collage of intercut news bulletins:

'The seventies punk rock band, The Dysfunckshonalz . . .'

'The police were called . . .'

'A hospital spokesman says . . .'

'And this year's King of the Jungle is . . .'

'And this year's Christmas number one is, you've guessed it, Billy Abortion, with his fantastic cover of Robbie Williams' "Angel" . . .'

Spotlight on Billy. The sound of a school choir singing the intro. As Billy is about to launch into the song, the sound of a needle scratching vinyl.

Blackout.